EDUCATION.

Sig. Head of Dept. Sr Marie Cecilia

Beginning Reading

Vera Southgate

 University of London Press Ltd

ISBN 0 340 15760 7 Boards
ISBN 0 340 15761 5 Unibook

University of London Press Ltd
St Paul's House, Warwick Lane, London EC4P 4AH

Printed in Great Britain by
Butler and Tanner Ltd, Frome and London

Contents

Acknowledgments

The author and publishers would like to thank the following for permission to include papers in this volume:

International Reading Association for two papers (Chapters 1 and 7), the first of which was published in Jenkinson, M. D. (ed.) (1967) *Reading Instruction: An International Forum* (Newark, Delaware, U.S.A.: International Reading Association), and the second presented at the Fifteenth Annual Convention of the Association at Anaheim, California, May 1970; United Kingdom Reading Association for four papers (Chapters 2, 3, 4, and 8) read at that Association's annual conferences and published in the conference proceedings—Downing, J. and Brown, A. L. (eds.) (1967) *The Second International Reading Symposium* (London: Cassell), Gardner, K. (ed.) (1970) *Reading Skills: Theory and Practice* (London: Ward Lock Educational), Brown, A. L. (ed.) (1967) *Reading: Current Research and Practice* (Edinburgh: Chambers), and Merritt, J. E. (ed.) (1971) *Reading and the Curriculum* (London: Ward Lock Educational), respectively; the Editors of *Educational Review* for a paper (Chapter 5) which has previously been printed in volume 16, number 1; and the National Foundation for Educational Research, Slough, for two papers (chapters 6 and 9) which have previously been printed in *Educational Research* (volume 7, number 2, and volume 11, number 1).

Introduction

From among the papers I have presented at various conferences and the articles I have written for different journals between 1963 and 1970, nine have been selected to form the content of this book. They are all concerned with beginning reading and each one forms a chapter of the book.

As an author I have found it interesting to look back over these articles and papers and remember how they came to be written. The two kinds of contributions occurred in different circumstances. Invitations to speak at international or national conferences frequently stated the topic or even the title to which one must speak. In these circumstances one was usually faced with a broad subject to be dealt with in a paper of limited length, say 3,000 words. This always represents a difficult task, and while engaged in it one often regrets having accepted the invitation. Nevertheless, on looking back, I now realize that some of my shorter and probably more lucid papers were produced in just that way, although at the time I chafed against the imposed limits which prevented me from expanding certain points as I should have liked.

Articles submitted to learned journals, on the other hand, generally arise in quite a different way. Normally one has an idea one considers important and one experiences a desire to communicate it to others. One is free from the constrictions of working on a prescribed topic, within a limited number of words and to meet a date deadline. There is an impetus and an involvement in such writing, as well as a measure of excitement in trying to present one's ideas to others. The result may be a freshness of approach, a liveliness which is often lacking in the formal paper, but, on the other hand, there may well be a verbosity through which, had it been disciplined, the message might have shone more clearly. Thus, on rereading certain of my articles and lectures where I was not restricted by a limit on length, while I can relive the fervour I felt at the time, I can also sympathize with the audience who had to suffer my verbosity!

Some of the nine papers and articles were written in the first person and some in the third person. The choice was not mine but was generally dictated by the editorial policy of the journal or by the procedures adopted by the conference committee concerned. Writing in the third person, of course, always appears more stilted than when the first person is used. Nevertheless, in this respect, the contributions in this book have been left as they were originally written. In fact, they are presented almost exactly in their original forms apart from a few minor amendments, such as the omission or reduction of certain passages which are developed in greater detail in other chapters. Where this has been done, cross-references are given.

Although the publications included in this book arose in different circumstances and are written in different forms, there is nevertheless a common theme running through them. Not only do they all refer to beginning reading, but my concern with particular aspects of the early stages of learning to read and the development of certain of my ideas can also be noted over the period of seven years during which these papers were written.

The contributions which form the book are grouped according to the subject matter, rather than being arranged chronologically. Part one is concerned with the 'how' and 'when' of beginning reading. Approaches to beginning reading in Britain are summarized in a paper I was invited to present to the First World Reading Conference in Paris in 1966. It is followed by a chapter on the ways in which a teacher might select an appropriate approach to beginning reading. Next the question of creating some structure in reading tuition in 'progressive' British primary schools is considered. Part One concludes with a summary of some of the arguments for and against early reading tuition.

Part Two of the book deals with new media for beginning reading. It begins with an account of my observations and testing of one of the first classes in Britain to use i.t.a. (or Augmented Roman Alphabet, as it was originally named). There follows a note of caution about interpreting the early i.t.a. results too optimistically: at the same time attention is drawn to the concept of a 'reading drive'. The third chapter in this section presents some of the main findings of the independent evaluation of i.t.a. which Professor F. W. Warburton and I undertook for the Schools Council. In the final chapter of Part Two, i.t.a. is compared with three colour codes.

The paper which forms Part Three of the book is entitled 'Formulae for Beginning Reading Tuition'. It commences by attempting to clarify and define some of the terminology currently in use with respect to beginning reading. (It may be that certain readers would prefer to examine the first few pages of Chapter 9 on 'Terminology' before reading the rest of the book.) The many dynamic factors at work within the classroom, which affect reading progress, are then considered and an order of priority is proposed. The reader will note that the selection of an approach to beginning reading is not regarded as the prime factor. Finally, the formula for beginning reading tuition which is developed leads to the suggestion that the designs of many experiments relating to different approaches to beginning reading are such that it is unlikely that their results will prove of practical value for teachers.

I trust that this book is one which both teachers and students will find useful, as it deals with many of the controversial issues that have arisen in the field of beginning reading in the past decade. I also hope that teachers will feel that during this period my attention has been centred on the real problems of the class teacher, and that I have been concerned about the teacher's practical problems relating to helping children to begin to read.

VERA SOUTHGATE

Part One   *How and when to begin*

1 Approaches to Beginning Reading in Great Britain

A paper presented at the First World Reading Conference, Paris, August 1966, and later published in Jenkinson, M. D. (ed.) 1967, READING INSTRUCTION: AN INTERNATIONAL FORUM.

I INTRODUCTION

It is a great honour and also a great responsibility to be invited to read a paper at this first World Reading Conference. I have found it difficult, just as I am sure my colleagues in this symposium have done, to condense such a large subject into a short paper. Furthermore, my paper is a purely personal appraisal of the situation, which might have appeared in a different light had it been presented by someone else. Consequently, over-simplification and subjectivity are likely to be two of the faults you will perceive in this description of approaches to beginning reading in Great Britain.

II BACKGROUND FACTORS

I should like to begin by outlining very briefly those background features of British education which appear to me to have particular relevance to our subject. Probably the two main points of interest to delegates from other countries are, first, the fact that compulsory schooling begins at the age of five and, secondly, the flexibility of our education system.

1.   *Infant classes*

The majority of children start school at the beginning of the term in which they will reach their fifth birthday. Infant education relates to children aged five to seven years and it is to this age range I shall be referring when considering beginning reading. Children spend between two and three years in infant schools, depending on the month in which they were born. The school day for infants lasts four and a half hours in Scotland and five hours in England and Wales, with a break at lunch-time.

A class is usually in the charge of the same teacher for the whole school day. Children's stay in a class can extend from a term to nearly three years, depending on the organization of the school. Boys and girls are taught in the same class. The average size of class is approximately 32 children, but the range extends from the permitted maximum of 40 to less than 20 pupils, with urban classes usually being much larger than rural classes. The age range of the children within a class varies from four months to almost three years.

2.   *The flexibility of British education*

The flexibility of British education requires stressing in connection with the teaching of reading. As an illustration of this point, it is worth noting that the Education Act of 1944, referring to children in England and Wales, does not even lay down that children should be taught to read.

Within their own schools headteachers enjoy almost complete autonomy. They are free to decide on the composition and organization of classes, the subjects to be included in the curriculum and the amount of time to be allocated to them. A headteacher may select any approach to reading he chooses, the grant of money for books and equipment being spent entirely at his discretion. Furthermore, it is important to note that although Her Majesty's Inspectors, representing the government, as well as local advisers and inspectors might offer advice in these areas, they would be unlikely, except in rare circumstances, to issue directives.

Headteachers quite often allow their staffs a large measure of freedom in questions of organization, books and methods. In consequence, the timing of the commencement of reading tuition, the choice of approach, the selection of books and the methods employed in beginning reading show as great a diversity as the organization, curriculum and time-tabling in infant classes.

III BEGINNING READING IN PRACTICE

1. *Beginning reading in a progressive school*

To obtain a fair picture of current reading practices in Great Britain, visitors from abroad would need to visit a number of different schools. However, let us begin by imagining that we are visiting what most educationists would consider to be a 'progressive' infant school.

The whole atmosphere of the school is informal and there is no division of the time-table into specific subjects to be taught. In the entrance hall and corridors we find lovely books, attractively displayed on shelves within children's reach. There are small chairs and tables where children can read or write. Pictures, flowers, nature-tables, a fish tank and displays of all kinds are in evidence. Every scrap of space is an extension of the stimulating environment which we find in the classrooms.

These classrooms seem to be bursting with Wendy houses, shops, post offices, work benches and facilities for experimenting with water, clay, paint and other creative materials. Labels and notices are attached to many of the activities. The walls of the rooms are covered with children's paintings, news sheets, charts and diagrams. Books are everywhere and there is a special book corner where children can read or browse quietly on their own. It is obvious that the teachers believe in 'creating an environment in which written language is a natural part', as suggested by the Ministry of Education (1959), and in which books are made to appear desirable to children.

Just as books spill out from the classrooms into the entrance hall and corridors, so do the children. We find them all over the school, busily engaged in a variety of activities, although apparently unsupervised. Some of these activities are concerned with reading and writing; others are not. There is an integrated approach to language and communication rather than an isolated approach to teaching reading. The first emphasis is on providing experiences which will encourage children to talk and so develop their spoken vocabulary.

The desire to communicate soon extends to writing. The five-year-old asks the teacher to write a title or a sentence on a picture he has painted. He copies it. This leads to simple news sheets and hand-made 'books' relating to the child's interests. Soon many five-year-olds can 'read' the captions on pictures and displays, the communal news sheets and simple hand-made books. At the same time, long before they can read published books, they are learning to handle them and enjoy them. The teacher frequently reads to the children and together they examine and discuss the books.

We find that some five-year-olds have progressed to the stage of reading easy published books and by the age of seven nearly all children are reading books *at some level*. These books include easy reference books, information books and picture dictionaries, as well as story books. Throughout this infant school we notice an emphasis on the enjoyment of reading and we see children doing a great deal of free writing. Most children have written many small books of stories they have invented or on topics which interested them, and some have written verse.

2. *Infant teachers—their training and beliefs*

Not all schools are like the one we have just visited. A glance at the training of teachers and their beliefs will help to illuminate the practices adopted in many schools. One important point should be noted; our infant teachers are not trained as reading specialists. In colleges where infant teachers are trained, the time spent on courses in reading and the content of the courses varies considerably. Moreover, an educational climate which leans towards an integrated approach to learning for young children, as is the case in Britain today, is unlikely to emphasise specific instruction in reading in the training of teachers. The result is that infant teachers, on leaving college, have some knowledge of child development and general theories of learning, a little theoretical knowledge of reading, a nodding acquaintance with certain of the current approaches to reading and a limited practical experience of using one or two reading approaches with children. They are unlikely to have studied closely such aspects as reading readiness, visual and auditory discrimination, testing and diagnostic work or programme planning for the mastery of specific skills. Our various systems of training students to teach reading may be described as general and intuitive rather than specific and scientific.

Not all infant classes, however, are staffed by teachers whose particular training was for infants. Some infant schools also contain teachers trained for older children, as well as part-time teachers and perhaps even a few untrained teachers. Moreover, we do not have reading specialists as advisers or consultants. On the other hand, some experienced heads and teachers can fairly claim to have become specialists in reading and part of their skill is inevitably shared with less-experienced colleagues.

Despite not being trained as reading specialists, most infant teachers consider learning to read to be extremely important. It is not uncommon to hear primary school advisers and inspectors expressing regret that our infant teachers are too 'reading-conscious'. Even when teachers believe in an informal approach to learning, it takes courage and confidence to delay the beginning of formal reading. Realizing the importance of reading, and believing that learning to read requires hard work, teachers are often anxious to make a beginning in order to see demonstrable results.

3. *Common practices in beginning reading*

Reading practices in Scotland and Wales differ somewhat from those in England. The Scottish Education Department (1955), for instance, states unequivocally that, 'The teaching of reading is one of the fundamental duties of the primary schools.' Reading tuition tends to begin earlier in Scotland, to be taught more formally, with greater emphasis on phonics and on reading aloud and with less accent on the development of creative writing alongside reading, than in England. Welsh schools are generally more formal than the most progressive of English infant schools. In addition, a proportion of Welsh schools have the problem of bilingualism.

The consequences of regional differences and of teachers' varied training and beliefs are that many schools in Britain differ from the progressive school we visited. Some are run on more formal lines. The mode of reading instruction extends from rather formal teaching to extremely informal learning situations. Class teaching is rare; individual instruction or guidance is more common. The most usual form of classroom organization in the language skills is represented by small, fairly fluid groups of children of similar reading attainment, working together.

Dependence on a basic reading scheme varies, with only a minority of teachers dispensing entirely with a published scheme. Nearly every school has supplementary books available for the children, but the quantity and quality of them is not uniform nor is the manner in which they are used. British reading schemes are less comprehensive than American schemes and generally have less supporting material, particularly in the form of work books. Even so, a proportion of British infant schools do not purchase all the supplementary materials available. The basic books have a steeper gradient and fewer repetitions of new words than many American books. The teacher's manuals for British schemes rarely provide detailed guidance for teaching. In any event, teachers do not always read the manuals, often preferring to utilize the books according to their own ideas.

The most usual procedure is for most teachers of five-year-olds to carry out a few activities designed to prepare children for reading, for instance such as those listed in Gray (1956). Very soon however, and probably too soon in the case of slower children, more direct teaching begins. With a look-and-say approach, the initial words of the scheme are introduced to small groups of children. Flash-card practice, possibly in the form of games, takes place. Introduction of the first book soon follows; the teacher's main mode of instruction being to 'hear the child read' and prompt him when he fails to read a word. If the basic scheme is phonic, then the teacher is likely to encourage the child to 'sound' unknown words, instead of prompting him. The teacher's principal aim is usually to help children to get through the basic scheme as quickly as possible. With a look-and-say scheme, some phonic work may be introduced when children reach the second or third book but it is not necessarily systematic. It is unusual to find a teacher who has planned a detailed reading programme, divided into specific categories of reading skills and with arrangements being made for graded instruction and guided practice at different levels.

4. Published approaches in use

British teachers tend to be rather conservative in their selection of approaches to reading and so the range of basic schemes changes slowly. The most popular are two look-and-say schemes published more than 10 years ago: *The Happy Venture Readers* (Schonell 1938) and *Janet and John* (O'Donnell and Munro 1949).[1] Much less popular, although fairly widely used, are two schemes which emphasise phonics: *The Beacon Readers* (Grassam 1957) and *Vanguard Readers* (Kettles and MacDonald 1949), the former being more widely used in England and the latter in Scotland. Most of the basic schemes published in the past ten years or so employ look-and-say sentence or word methods. Examples of such schemes are *Queensway Reading* (Brearley and Neilson 1964), *The Happy Trio Reading Scheme* (Gray *et al.* 1956), *The McKee Readers* (McKee *et al.* 1956), *Key Words Reading Scheme* (Murray 1964), *Ready To Read Scheme* (Simpson 1966) and *Let's Learn to Read* (Taylor and Ingleby 1960).

One scheme, *The Royal Road Readers* (Daniels and Diack 1957) relies on a 'phonic word method'. The past decade in Britain has also seen the beginning of a movement towards some systematic phonic training, with an increase in the publication of phonic books and apparatus meant to be used alongside look-and-say schemes. The following are examples of phonic supplementary materials: *Six Phonic Workbooks* (Grassam 1966), *A Remedial Reading Method* (Moxon 1962), *Sounds for Reading* (O'Donnell and Munro 1965), *Fun with Phonics* (Reis 1962), *Sounds and Words* (Southgate and Havenhand 1959), *Programmed Reading Kit* (Stott 1962), *Sound Sense* (Tansley 1961) and *Practical Reading: Some New Remedial Techniques* (Webster 1965).

The general acceptance of a combination of look-and-say

1 For this and other numbered notes, see 'Addenda' at the ends of each chapter.

methods with some phonic training reflects the nature of our
written language, with its combination of phonically regular
words and irregular words. As a result of the irregularity, the
beginning reader never knows whether an unknown word is one
he should try to 'sound' himself or one about which he should
consult his teacher. Two new approaches available in Britain try
to overcome this difficulty by presenting the beginner with a
regular code or series of signals. The Initial Teaching Alphabet,
usually known as i.t.a., consists of an augmented alphabet of
44 characters; in contrast, in *Words in Colour* (Gattegno 1962)
each sound has been allocated a colour, regardless of its particular
spelling in different words. Each code, in effect, indicates to the
child, 'Whenever you see *this* (be it a written symbol or a colour),
you say *this* sound.' The learner is thus enabled to develop a
consistent method of attacking new words. Both the new alphabet and the coloured letters are temporary props for beginning
reading, intended to be dropped as children gain fluency.

   Words in Colour, in addition to introducing a colour code,
also advocates quite formal teaching methods, reminiscent of old-
fashioned drill with phonic word lists. Most British infant teachers
find these suggested methods unpalatable. Accordingly, this
approach is being used in only a few infant classes.

   In contrast, the use of i.t.a. with infants has spread fairly
rapidly. In *i.t.a. Journal, No. 9* (1966) it is stated that 1,517 schools
are now using it.[2] The figure probably represents approximately
5% of all infant schools in Britain. The fairly rapid increase in
the use of i.t.a. may, I believe, be attributed to five main factors.
First, it has received more publicity than any new approach to
reading in Britain has ever received. Secondly, when it was introduced, no changes in methods of teaching were advocated.
Thirdly, teachers feel that its comparative regularity has reduced
what they described as 'the grind' of learning to read, thus making
the task easier and happier for both themselves and the children.
Fourthly, its introduction has often been accompanied by increases
in the quantity and quality of children's free writing. Finally,
most teachers who have used it have found it functionally commendable and have recommended it to other teachers.

   Some experiments are being carried out along the lines of

programmed learning and with audio-visual aids for beginning reading. Only a few, of which *Programmed Reading* (Sullivan 1963) is one, are at present generally available in Great Britain. *The S.R.A. Reading Laboratories* (Parker 1958), have provided our first taste of 'multilevel, developmental reading improvement programmes'. Not many of these laboratories are being tried out in infant classes; those in use have been introduced mainly to older children. Linguistic approaches to beginning reading have not yet arrived in Britain. I suspect that those now being published in the U.S.A., which commence with lists of dull phonic words, are unlikely to appeal to our infant teachers. On the other hand, the use of programmed reading texts and reading laboratories may well increase as, not only do they follow the trend I have suggested towards more specific training but, at the same time, they cater for individual needs. It may also be that the experiments with i.t.a. will crystallize dissatisfaction with the irregularities of our orthography, so that attention is turned towards simplified spelling systems and codes such as diacritical marks or colours.

IV   THE RESULTS OF OUR APPROACHES TO BEGINNING
     READING

Current approaches to beginning reading in Great Britain are very closely linked with three facets of our educational system: the permissiveness which contrasts markedly with the education regulations of many other countries, children's entry to full-time schooling at the age of five, and the absence of reading specialists.

Flexibility, linked with the fact of non-specialist teachers, has both strengths and weaknesses. The following are among the advantages. First, the teacher is interested in the development of the whole child and not merely in teaching a subject. Secondly, freedom for both teacher and pupil increases motivation and interest. Thirdly, when reading and writing spring from the total life of the school, they spread throughout the day and are consequently reinforced in many different situations.

Some possible disadvantages are as follows. It requires a

skilled teacher, who really knows the children in her care, to handle effectively the learning situation depicted in the progressive, informal class. To judge when each child is ready to begin to read and to ensure that guidance, instruction and practice are applied at the appropriate moments within the informal setting is not an easy task. These difficulties are increased when staff changes are numerous. In such situations two serious dangers may arise. Slower children might be forced to make a too-early start with reading, resulting in the development of adverse attitudes which could prevent them from learning to read even at a later age. Secondly, in the acquisition of the skill, certain areas of reading development might receive scant attention.

In practice, however, our permissive and intuitive approaches to beginning reading are much more successful than delegates working under more formal educational systems might imagine, although I should certainly not claim that they are entirely satisfactory.

Those of you who are curious or sceptical about our children beginning school at five must wonder about their reading attainments at seven. Unfortunately a short paper does not permit one to list many research results. Briefly, the results of various surveys of six-, seven- and eight-year-olds, for example, Kellmer Pringle (1957), Scholl (1960) and Taylor (1950), comparing British children with American children who start school approximately a year later, suggest that British children read better sooner than American children, with greater gains on word recognition than on reading comprehension tests. Anderson (1964) testing Scottish, English and American children found that, at the age of seven, the British children excelled American children of the same age in a variety of reading, writing and spelling tests. The advantages decreased with age, until at ages 11 and 14 the British children only retained advantages in spelling and word meaning tests.

An investigation into the books which children are actually reading at seven plus, reveals that some children have made practically no progress in reading. Morris (1959) reported that in 1954 in Kent (England) 19% of seven-year-old children were still at the stage of the first primer or below it. However, the Ministry of Education's (1957) survey indicated that reading standards were rising. My own impression is that if a similar survey were carried out today there would be a reduction in this percentage of slow readers.

But test scores are rarely adequate as assessments of results in our modern infant classes. They only tell us a fraction of the story. We need to visit the schools and observe that by the age of seven plus nearly all children have begun to learn to read. Most of them are confident and independent children who enjoy reading at their own levels. In particular I should like you to see the five-year-olds—the many who *want* to learn to read, their eagerness to start, their pride and enjoyment in beginning to acquire the skill and their delight in demonstrating it. Teachers, as well as visitors, are almost pestered by young children eager to read to them. I hope that many of you may soon be among such visitors to British infant schools.

V   SUMMING UP

1.   British teachers cherish their freedom to employ any approach to beginning reading which they consider appropriate.

2.   This flexibility in our educational system generates a vitality and motivation in both teachers and pupils which usually makes beginning reading a joyous and exciting process.

3.   On the other hand, the selection of an appropriate approach, the decision about when individual children are ready to begin, as well as the detailed planning required to achieve mastery of the various skills which comprise the total skill of reading, all demand a special expertise on the part of the teacher.

4.   This expertise could be increased if teachers received a more specific and specialized training in reading than at present.

5.   Most children of five are eager to begin to read and many are capable of doing so.

6.   By the age of seven plus, 'Some (children) read fluently and with deep absorption; many can use books to find out what they want to know. All but a very few will have made a start in reading' (Ministry of Education 1959). This reading skill will have developed alongside the other language skills and usually without

neglect of mathematics, music-making, exploration of the environment and creative activities which form by far the largest part of our infant's day.

ADDENDA

1. Goodacre (1967), reporting on the basic reading schemes used in 100 primary schools in London in 1958–61, found that 62 schools used mainly *Janet and John*, 15 schools relied on *Happy Venture* and another 15 schools on *Beacon*.

2a. Warburton and Southgate (1969) in *i.t.a.: An Independent Evaluation*, the report of a study carried out for the Schools Council, reported that in 1966, 9.2% of all the schools in England and Wales containing infant pupils were using i.t.a. to some extent with infants, a total of 1,554 schools.

b. In *Trends in Education*, 20 (October 1970), the quarterly journal produced by the Department of Education and Science, 'Question Master', referring to i.t.a. in 'Talking Point', states, 'There are now about 3,000 schools using it—one-sixth of the total number of infant schools and infant departments.'

2 Selecting an Approach to Teaching Reading

A paper[1] presented at the Second Annual Conference of the United Kingdom Reading Association, London, July 1965, and later published in Downing, J. and Brown, A. L. (eds.) 1967 THE SECOND INTERNATIONAL READING SYMPOSIUM.

I TEACHERS' INTEREST IN NEW APPROACHES

One of the most endearing characteristics of teachers is that they rarely feel they know all the answers. This is particularly true in the field of reading where, however good the work they are doing, teachers are frequently dissatisfied with the progress of their pupils. Teachers' great interest in reading is continually being demonstrated by the large numbers of them who attend courses and conferences concerned with reading. I have often wondered why this should be so. It is probably due partly to teachers' beliefs that reading is a basic skill, as well as to the fact that parents expect that their children will learn to read at school and this expectancy is reflected in the children. One other reason suggests itself. Teachers, particularly those in charge of young children, undertake a variety of tasks calling for continuous and painstaking training of their pupils. The results of much of this training are difficult to assess and, consequently, satisfaction for teachers is frequently in the far-distant future. Teaching children to read, on the other hand, is one of the teacher's tasks which gives tangible results.

Their strong urge to help children to learn to read causes

teachers to look hopefully at new approaches* to reading. (In this paper I am using the phrase 'new approaches' in a very broad sense to mean new reading schemes, new sets of apparatus or equipment, new methods* or more often variations in former methods, as well as new media.*) No teacher can afford entirely to ignore the many new reading schemes or ideas on the teaching of reading which are continually being published, each of which is likely to be advanced as the panacea for all reading failure. The authors, the originators of ideas, the experimenters and the enthusiastic practitioners generally claim marvellous results. Consequently the teacher, reading reports of these experiments, can soon believe that any one of them is the answer to all her† own reading problems. I do not for one moment suggest that the claims made are false. Indeed, I wholeheartedly believe in them— in all of them! I have achieved such results myself with new ideas of my own, as well as with approaches devised by other people. On visits to a large variety of schools I have also observed good results being attained by using different methods and different schemes. In addition, I frequently receive letters from teachers who have experimented with new ways of teaching reading, telling me of the acceleration in their pupils' reading progress. Such claims can usually be accepted as valid, although those making the claims may not always be correct in attributing the results to the methods or reading materials used rather than to themselves.

The danger for the teacher is that when she reads of the progress which has been made by pupils who have used this or that published scheme, she may become convinced that she is not using 'the best method' or 'the best reading scheme' with her pupils, and that only a new set of books or reading apparatus will lead to the desired progress. Yet, not surprisingly when one considers the number of claims which are published, the teacher often feels bewildered by the choice. I am reminded of the reports in experimental psychology in which animals are exposed to situations in which a choice must be made. When the alternatives

* Definitions of terminology relating to beginning reading are given in Chapter 9, pages 138–9.

† As the majority of teachers concerned with beginning reading are infant teachers, most of whom are female, throughout this book the teacher is referred to as 'she' while the child is referred to as 'he'

offered are widely dissimilar the choice is comparatively simple. As the alternatives become more and more alike the animal finds itself unable to make a choice. Continued exposure to this difficult situation is likely to produce in the animal a condition equivalent to a nervous breakdown in a human being.

I do not wish to imply that teachers of reading are in imminent danger of nervous breakdowns, but merely that the rival claims of many new approaches to reading are so similar that the teacher may be too bewildered to make a rational choice. Furthermore, it is not as easy as it might appear for the teacher to obtain all the relevant information about the different schemes in order to make a critical appraisal of them. Publishers are not always willing or able to send complete reading schemes or bulky boxes of apparatus to schools for inspection purposes. Even when publishers do cooperate in this way, the work of examining specimen books and equipment is increased by the task of parcelling and returning them.

The problem of the choice of an approach to beginning reading is a very real one to the teacher and it is a growing problem. In my attempt to give some guidance on the subject I shall first suggest that the selection of a new approach to reading is not necessarily the only answer to the teacher's problems. The fact that children's reading progress is not as good as the teacher desires may not be attributable to the books and apparatus which are being used or even to the main teaching method in the school. Secondly, I shall go on to indicate that if a new approach is required there are certain useful criteria on which its selection may be based.

II   IS A NEW APPROACH NECESSARY?

Teachers who are anxious to effect improvements in their pupils' reading standards almost invariably ask the question, 'Which is the best reading scheme or method to use?' There are two assumptions here: first, that there is a definite answer to this question as one scheme or method has been proved to be 'the best'; and, second, that this is the key question in the reading situation. Neither of these assumptions appears to me to be true.

In the first place, research results which will give us clear answers on this point are just not available. Furthermore, I think it is highly unlikely that one method or scheme will ever prove equally effective for all pupils, being taught by all teachers, in all situations.

The second assumption, that the choice of method or scheme is the most important factor in the teaching of reading, is one which my experience has led me to question. I have come to believe that the teacher herself is at least equally as important as the approach, and probably even more important. During my teaching experience in different schools, I quite often found that the reading scheme in use in my class was not one which I would have selected. Yet, whichever scheme it happened to be and however much I despaired of it, I found that once I really set about teaching reading, good progress was made. Experience in charge of a remedial and advisory service also showed me that different remedial teachers using various schemes and methods produced equally good results.

Observation of reading teaching in schools of all types revealed good standards being attained by extremely formal methods in some schools, as well as by informal methods in other schools; at the same time both formal and informal methods failed lamentably in certain schools. I can also recall schools which must be rated as comparable as far as buildings and equipment, intelligence of the children, socio-economic background and staffing are concerned, and where the same reading schemes are in use; yet one such school has high reading standards while the other has poor standards. The salient factors here are surely the beliefs, attitudes and drive of the teachers rather than the schemes or methods being used. Finally, I have seen remarkable reading progress when some alteration has been made in the school situation other than changing the books or the method. To give only a few examples: the grouping or cross-classification of children for teaching reading, a reorganization of all the reading books in the school, staff discussions resulting in detailed planning to prevent and overcome reading problems, have all been observed to result in increased performance.

These experiences have led me to develop the concept of a

reading drive.* It consists mainly of interest in and enthusiasm for the teaching of reading on the part of the teacher. This enthusiasm is coupled with a happy rather than a grim determination that children will make progress and it fills the teacher with a surge of inspiration and energy for the task. I am convinced that when teachers are interested and enthusiastic, the *teaching of reading takes place* and children usually do learn to read. Thus I suggest that a reading drive in any school can raise reading standards considerably, even without the purchase of new books and equipment. This does not mean that additions to the reading materials in a school are to be despised, but merely that in the past too much attention may have been given to the new approaches and too little to the drive, enthusiasm and interest of the teacher.

If my insistence on a reading drive has given the impression that I do not consider new approaches to the teaching of reading important, then I must hasten to correct myself. What I am trying to emphasize is that without reading drive in the school, no new approach is likely to succeed. The apathetic teacher will not do well with any reading approach, while the keen reading teacher will succeed despite inadequate reading materials. Even so, the teacher who possesses reading drive cannot fail to be interested in, and even excited about, the many new approaches now being developed. Such a teacher is bound to be eager to examine and try out some of the new schemes, so let us consider how the choice may be made.

III CRITERIA FOR JUDGING NEW APPROACHES

Within the total problem of learning to read four main factors may be discerned: the task, the learner, the teacher, and theories of learning; the latter point being inextricably interwoven with the preceding three points. If, in drawing up criteria for assessing new approaches to reading, I seem to be placing the greatest emphasis on the teacher it is not because I consider the three remaining factors unimportant. It is merely that in a short paper it would be

* A more detailed discussion of 'reading drive' is given in Chapter 6, pages 87–93.

impossible to discuss all the factors fully, and also that I suspect that the teacher, who generally receives least attention, may well be the most important factor in the situation.

Three main decisions need to be taken in the choice of an approach to reading. The first decision concerns basic beliefs about learning to read, the second concerns the main methods of teaching reading, and the third decision relates to specific approaches. It is important that all three decisions should be taken, and in the suggested order.

The first decision is the one most frequently ignored. It involves a choice between two main philosophies of helping children to learn to read. I would describe these broad approaches as 'incidental learning' and 'systematic teaching'. The teacher who supports the first philosophy believes that children will learn to read if they are placed in a stimulating environment, if they participate in interesting activities and if they are surrounded by books and given the right sort of encouragement at the right time. In such a class the early reading vocabulary of the children will spring mainly from the children's own spoken and written language, relating to the everyday activities of the classroom. In the early stages, few published reading books may be used as children will be making their own simple books using words connected with their own interests. Later, the teacher's belief in a free choice of reading materials may result in the children dipping into a variety of reading schemes. If a basic reading scheme is used, it is probably look-and-say rather than phonic.

The teacher who supports the second philosophy believes that reading is a skill which can, and should, be taught systematically. Such a teacher is likely to base the reading tuition on one of the published reading schemes or, less frequently, on a detailed teaching programme of her own. The published reading scheme may be phonic rather than look-and-say, although a look-and-say scheme can be used successfully by someone who believes in systematic teaching. In the latter case, the child would be taught the basic sight vocabulary, probably by games and other activities, before he encountered the words in the book, as opposed to merely being prompted by the teacher every time he failed to read a word. Follow-up activities would be planned and phonic training would be likely to be introduced at some stage. The hallmark of the systematic teaching outlook is that both the teaching and the learning are part of a planned reading programme and they take place regularly rather than spasmodically.

In general, the more informal classroom situations and look-and-say approaches tend to be associated with the first teacher and the slightly more formal classroom routine and phonic approaches with the second teacher but these are only very broad classifications. The demarcation between these two philosophies is by no means rigid; there is a good deal of overlap. Some teachers who would describe themselves as believing in systematic teaching may, in practice, not carry this out. On the other hand, the good teacher in the incidental learning category may do far more formal teaching or arrange far more guided learning than is apparent. In such a class the teaching is usually with individual children or with small groups of children, as the need arises; hence it is not necessarily systematic.

Quite clearly a teacher's basic beliefs about learning to read exert a vital influence on every aspect of her handling of the subject. It is for this reason that it is essential for the teacher who is considering a new approach to reading to decide first whether her beliefs lean towards 'incidental learning' or 'systematic teaching'. Once this decision has been reached, a framework is available against which to consider the second question.

The second question concerns which of the main methods or what combination of methods the teacher will adopt. This problem is created partly by the nature of our written language. There are contradictions in the printed symbols in that, on the one hand, the same letters do not always represent the same sounds and, on the other hand, the same sounds can be represented by a variety of different letters or combinations of letters. Broadly speaking, in our language we have two kinds of words; first, those which follow specific rules although there are exceptions to the rules, and secondly, words which are quite irregular—and many of our more commonly used words fall into this category. Consequently, in the past, we have had two broad approaches to the teaching of reading: phonic methods with an emphasis on words that follow fairly well defined rules, and look-and-say methods which rely heavily on memorizing irregular words as sight patterns. Of course these two methods overlap. Because of the nature of our language neither method can operate entirely without the other. The phonic scheme must use some basic sight words, and many of the look-and-say schemes, at some stage, point out or introduce phonic rules. The majority of teachers are inclined to claim that they use a combination of these two methods.

Recently, however, we have become aware of a possible way of overcoming the problem created by the irregularities of English; namely, by the adoption of a regular and purely temporary code of sound-symbol relationships for the initial stages of learning to read. Two recent approaches to beginning reading, i.t.a.* and *Words in Colour** (Gattegno 1962), although I am aware that their different supporters would not like to have them classed together in this manner, nevertheless share one common feature: they are designed, each in its different way, to provide children with a uniform method of deciphering unknown words.

Only when the teacher has taken the first decision about a basic philosophy, followed by the second decision about a main method, will she be ready to examine particular approaches with the needs of her pupils in mind. It would be ideal if we were now able to consider a number of new approaches in detail, but unfortunately there is not time. Furthermore, both American and British teachers are present at this conference and, while a few reading schemes and approaches are common to both countries, the approaches generally available in the two countries are different. Accordingly, to help you to answer the third question I postulated, I have summarized on the duplicated sheets† which have been distributed some of the points which a teacher might bear in mind when appraising particular approaches to reading. These notes certainly do not form a complete list of all possible criteria for the selection of a reading approach, but they will serve to remind you of some of the points I have made and to suggest

---

* These two approaches have already been mentioned in Chapter 1, page 20, and are compared more fully in Chapter 8, pages 116–34.

† A copy of these notes is included at the end of this chapter, commencing on page 33.

further points which there has not been time to raise. Perhaps we might now discuss some of the suggestions in this list; the remainder you may like to consider at your leisure.

IV SUMMARY OF CONCLUSIONS

New approaches to the teaching of reading, many of them supported by reports of excellent results, continually confront the teacher. As a consequence teachers may begin to believe that an entirely new approach is a prerequisite to the acceleration of their pupils' reading progress; yet the wide range of new ideas makes the ideal choice extremely difficult.

I have suggested that a new approach is not necessarily the answer to all reading problems. It may well be that the teacher is more important than either the reading materials or the method and thus a reading drive may achieve good results without a change in either. Should a new approach be deemed necessary, I have put forward the view that three main decisions need to be taken in its selection. First, the teacher needs to decide on her basic philosophy about learning to read—'incidental learning' or 'systematic teaching'. Secondly, the teacher needs to choose a main method or one of the newer approaches which seeks to eliminate, in the early stages of learning to read, the inconsistencies in our written language. Only at this stage should the third decision concerning particular approaches be attempted, and I have listed certain criteria against which reading schemes and apparatus might be appraised.

(NOTE: *The following is a copy of the duplicated notes distributed to conference members.*)

POINTS FOR CONSIDERATION WHEN EXAMINING READING SCHEMES, BOOKS AND APPARATUS

A *The teacher's point of view*

1. What are the teacher's basic beliefs about children learning to read—'incidental learning', or 'systematic teaching'?

2. What are the headteacher's beliefs and consequently the 'climate' of the school?

3. What is the classroom organization within which the teacher feels able to do the best work? Is it basically formal or informal? Will the reading approach fit into this framework?

4. Does the approach fit in with what the teacher believes about the ways in which children learn?

e.g. If it is true that a child learns by doing, does the approach afford children the opportunity of being active in the learning situation?

5. Does the teacher want to be always initiating the teaching and learning, or does she want the scheme to encourage and cater for children working on their own?

6. Is the teacher looking for a complete basic reading scheme, an aid to an existing reading scheme, or supplementary books?

7. Is the teacher looking for an approach which is mainly look-and-say, phonic, a combination of both, or a new idea for simplifying the initial difficulties arising from the inconsistencies of our written language?

8. Does the teacher prefer written work to be incorporated in the scheme or not?

9. What is the range of reading attainments which the teacher is expecting the scheme to cater for?

10. How much will the new approach cost? (This figure requires working out in detail for each separate class, according to the various needs of the children in the class.)

B   *The needs of the children*

1. Number of children in the class?
2. Age range?
3. Intelligence?
4. Reading attainments?
5. Home backgrounds and interests?
6. Special problems of failing readers?

C   *The author's ideas*

1. *Read carefully the teacher's manual or the instructions.*

2.   Are the author's basic beliefs and aims in line with the teacher's?

3.   Alternatively, does the scheme or approach fulfil a need which the teacher has previously felt but perhaps not crystallized?

4.   Consider the background of the author of the scheme. For example, he may have had experience as a teacher of infants, juniors, illiterate adolescents or adults, or Educationally Sub-Normal children. If your pupils are not in the same category, has the author applied his principles successfully to the age-group and category of children you are teaching? If the author is not a teacher, but perhaps an educationist, a psychologist, or a linguistic expert, have his ideas been tried out in practical situations and have his principles been applied successfully to the kind of children with whom you are concerned?

D   *The books or schemes*

1.   Consider the presentation, interest, illustrations, vocabulary, print, length, size and durability of reading books.

2.   In look-and-say schemes, consider the vocabulary control in two ways:

a.   gradient of introduction of new words;

b.   the frequency of repetition of words.

3.   In look-and-say schemes, is there an abundance of suitable supplementary material?

4.   In phonic schemes, consider:

a.   the steepness of gradient in the introduction of rules;

b.   the opportunities for practising the rules, particularly in interesting and different situations;

c.   the opportunities for transferring the skills which are being acquired.

5.   Order the *entire* scheme, including *all* the supplementary books and *all* the apparatus.

6.   In the first instance, use the scheme as the author intended it to be used. (Until the teacher is thoroughly familiar with a scheme, it is unlikely that the innovations or omissions which she makes to a carefully planned reading programme will be in the nature of improvements.)

B

E *Apparatus*

The selection of reading apparatus poses special difficulties for the teacher. Many of the points given earlier in this list are relevant to the selection of reading apparatus, in addition to the following points.

1. Is there a teacher's manual or pamphlet which states precisely the author's aims in the production of the apparatus?
2. Is the apparatus intended as a complete scheme or as a supplement to other schemes?
3. If it is not complete in itself, does it really supplement your existing reading programme?
4. Are there detailed instructions to the teacher for using the apparatus?
5. Are the rules which the children must follow simple and clear?
6. Will the children actually *learn something* from using this apparatus or will it just occupy them?
7. Will it take a large amount of the teacher's time to prepare the apparatus, in the first instance, and then to arrange storage for it and organize it for each lesson?
8. Alternatively, is the apparatus designed so that the children can distribute, collect and store it satisfactorily?
9. Is the apparatus attractive and durable?
10. Is the apparatus *self-checking*, in some way, or will the children complete the task in a minute or two and then have to wait twenty minutes or so for the teacher to check it?
11. How many children does one set of apparatus cater for?
12. What will it cost to provide the apparatus for the class or group which is going to use it?

ADDENDUM

1. The ideas put forward in this paper were later expanded to form a book, published by University of London Press Ltd under the title of *Reading—Which Approach?* (Southgate and Roberts 1970).

3 The Importance of Structure in Beginning Reading

*A paper presented at the Sixth Annual Conference of the
United Kingdom Reading Association, Nottingham, July 1960;
and later published in Gardner, K. 1970* READING SKILLS:
THEORY AND PRACTICE.
*Some of the ideas contained in this paper had been mentioned
previously in a paper entitled 'Structuring reading materials
for beginning reading' presented at the Second World
Congress on Reading, Copenhagen, August 1968, and later
published in Staiger, R. C. and Andreson, O. (eds.) 1969*
READING: A HUMAN RIGHT AND A HUMAN PROBLEM.

I   READING IN PROGRESSIVE INFANT CLASSES

In primary education in Britain today the most noticeable trend
is towards what are usually termed 'progressive' schools or classes.
The keynotes of such schools are fluidity and informality in the
grouping of children and in time-tabling, freedom of movement,
individual choice of activities and discovery methods of learning.
In view of what follows in the remainder of this paper, I should
like to stress from the outset that I approve of this development
in primary education, with its emphasis on the child himself and
how he may learn rather than on the teacher's instruction.
Indeed, it would be difficult not to appreciate the opportunities
which such schools provide for highly motivated and purposeful
learning, for individual progress, for the development of independence, responsibility and attitudes of enquiry, for the encouragement of creativity and for social interaction.

On the other hand, I am seriously concerned by the fact that the movement towards child-centred learning in progressive schools is frequently accompanied by a decline in the belief of the importance of young children learning to read. The Plowden Report (Department of Education and Science 1967), for example, very clearly reflects this attitude. In this 500-page report covering all aspects of primary education, only five pages deal specifically with reading, and of these only one page relates to 'Teaching Children to Read'. This is certainly a far cry from the time when the work of the primary school was centred on the 'Three Rs'. While one would not wish to advocate a return to such concentration on 'Three R' work, I fear that we are in danger of going too far in the opposite direction. I still consider that one of the main functions of primary education should be in the inculcation of literacy. Accordingly, we should guard against any tendency to believe that it is less important for young children to learn to read and write than it is for them to learn about mathematics and science or for them to have opportunities to express themselves, to create and to discover.

The current deprecation of the importance of learning to read is accompanied by a swing in emphasis from teaching to learning. 'Progressive' teachers try to avoid the use of the phrase 'teaching children to read', and to replace it with some such phrase as 'providing an environment in which children will be encouraged to learn to read'. A wide variety of books, which the teacher reads to the children and which they freely handle, reading apparatus, paper and pencils, all form important parts of this environment. These teachers believe that in such a situation children will soon want to learn to read and, with a little encouragement and guidance, will succeed in doing so.

Both the older approach to reading tuition, that of systematically planned instruction, and the newer theory of incidental learning contain inherent dangers. When teachers pin their faith on instruction, the grave danger is that they may assume that what has been taught has also been learned. One has only to observe either class or group reading instruction taking place, to realize the fallacy of this assumption. The proportion of pupil time devoted to features of the environment other than the teacher or the task, and likewise the proportion of the teacher's time devoted to attempts to focus children's attention on her instruction, increases rapidly as the lesson proceeds.

In contrast, when the emphasis is on learning, the main danger is that the teacher will assume that in a stimulating environment, with freedom to explore and experiment, all children will eventually want to learn to read, and will be able to so without direct instruction. Brighter pupils or those from homes in which literacy is valued frequently do so. Yet I am certain that many other children will fail to learn to read in infant classes unless a good deal of guidance and instruction is undertaken by the teacher. There are some children who would be neither 'motivated' nor 'ready' by the time that they were eight or nine or ten, if someone did not do something about it. The situation is somewhat similar to that of children learning to eat green vegetables or salads; many would never do so unless adults encouraged them to try, and fed them with small initial doses.

Furthermore, I do not see why it should be assumed that it is bad for young children to do some directed work. On the contrary, children both want and enjoy a certain amount of direct teaching and systematic practice. It would be a pity if teachers were to reach the stage when they become almost ashamed of doing some teaching. Yet this situation is in sight. I have been in infant schools where teachers apologize when one finds them actually teaching a small group of children; they hasten to assure one that this is exceptional!

It is also interesting to note that many of the strongest supporters of the incidental learning theory are advisers, inspectors, lecturers or writers on infant education; in other words, those who do not have to cope with the aftermath, in junior classes and remedial groups, of children who have been left in infant classes to explore the reading environment. Such children have more often ignored or floundered in the reading environment than explored it purposefully.

Nevertheless, there is no doubt that the good teacher in the informal infant class does manage to ensure that each child makes progress in reading, according to his individual needs and abilities, in ways which might be described as 'incidental learning'. Close observation in such a class, however, would show the experienced teacher to be structuring the learning situation for the individual child, and particularly for the slower child. It would be seen that both individual diagnosis and planned learning were being carried out intuitively and functionally by this teacher, and that individual records of children's progress were being kept. Ensuring reading progress for all children in these conditions, however, is an extraordinarily difficult task, and younger, less experienced, or less able teachers are not always able to succeed.

II   THE NEED FOR STRUCTURE

I have three main reasons for believing in the need for structure in beginning reading tuition. In the first place, written English does not constitute a regular spelling system. If the written form of our language represented a one-to-one relationship between written symbol and spoken sound, we might have a reasonable basis for hoping that, by heuristic methods, children could be encouraged to discover these relationships and so form generalizations. But our spelling system actually prevents children from making generalizations. For example, the child who has just begun to form a mental concept of the letter *a* after meeting it in 'cat', 'man', and 'bag', will quickly have his theory demolished when he comes across words such as 'cake', 'father' or 'water'. Such a situation not only discourages the child from trying to discover things for himself, but makes it practically impossible for him to do so. Discovery methods in the fields of mathematics and science are more practical propositions, for here there are regular rules waiting to be discovered. Given sufficient opportunities and encouragement in the appropriate environment, which contains a wealth of carefully structured equipment, brighter children are able to explore these subjects by heuristic methods. Yet it should be noted, in passing, that certain teachers are already realizing that slower children make little progress in discovering for themselves even the unalterable laws of mathematics and science without a great deal of teacher guidance, as well as a certain amount of direct instruction.

Secondly, discovery methods of learning, to be effective, require certain basic skills of which reading is probably the most important, followed closely by the knowledge of how to use an index, simple dictionaries and reference books. While it is true that young children, even before they have started to read and write, can begin to discover, observe, experiment and compare, their progress is necessarily limited by lack of these skills. Thus heuristic methods of learning will be greatly facilitated, and can only be fully developed, when children are able to read and write.

Thirdly, the staffing position in our primary schools today presents a picture of constantly changing members of staff. The newly trained teacher is often in schools only two or three years before she is married and leaving to have a family. Older married women return to teaching when the youngest of their children have started school, which may be after absences of fifteen or more years. There is also a floating population of temporary teachers. The older, experienced infant teacher is frequently the exception rather than the rule. This pattern of changing staffs in primary schools seems likely to continue. It has already been suggested that the informal infant class is far from easy to handle, and that mastery of the printed and written forms of our language represents a difficult task. In these circumstances, continuity in reading tuition is unlikely to be achieved for individual children if learning to read is an informal, often haphazard, feature of the school environment. New members of staff will be greatly helped, and children's reading progress more easily ensured, within a planned reading programme based on a certain amount of structured reading materials.

It is not always realized that the meticulous planning of a framework for learning to read does not have to be accompanied by formalized instruction. Indeed, I should go so far as to say that the reverse is true. My observations and experience in infant classes have led me to conclude that the freer the atmosphere and the more informal the working procedures, the more imperative it becomes that the reading environment should be so structured as not only to encourage reading but also to forward its progress.

III   STRUCTURING THE READING ENVIRONMENT

In the past ten years or so, in contrast to the growth of 'progressive' primary schools, there has been a noticeable movement towards structured reading materials and procedures. This trend can be seen in a re-emphasis on phonics; in an awareness of the contribution of linguistics to reading tuition; in the publication of equipment such as Sullivan's (1963) *Programmed Reading* and the *S.R.A. Reading Laboratories* (Parker 1958); in the introduction of new media; and in the growing interest in teaching machines and programmes for reading tuition. Teachers in progressive primary schools have usually stood aside from this stream of thought. My contention is that progressive teachers, even more than relatively formal teachers, should give serious consideration to this movement towards structure. I am certain that if they would examine, adapt and incorporate into their progressive schools some of these forms of structuring, the reading and writing as well as other work in the school would benefit.

In this paper I shall limit myself to a discussion of only three of the many areas within the total reading environment which may be restructured in such a way as to facilitate the acquisition of beginning reading skills. The first relates to either regularizing the written code or drawing attention to the regularities within it which already exist. The second entails devising a master plan of reading tuition, with built-in diagnostic and recording devices. The third concerns the selection, organization and use of reading materials in a manner designed to further the master plan. I shall only touch on the first two points and devote the majority of my time in this lecture to presenting you with samples of reading materials to illustrate the third point.

1.   *Structuring the written code*

Most practising teachers of beginning reading are well aware of those difficulties, caused by the irregularities of the English system of spelling, which children experience when they first try to read. Our efforts to ease this burden may turn in either of two directions. We can either carefully consider the new media for beginning reading which are advocated or we can concentrate on ways of emphasizing the regularities of the language.

One of the most noticeable innovations in beginning reading materials in recent years has been the introduction of a variety of regularized codes. We have had, among others, *i.t.a.* (Pitman 1959), *Words in Colour* (Gattegno 1962), *Diacritical Marking System* (Fry 1967), *Colour Story Reading* (Jones 1967) and *Reading by Rainbow* (Bleasdale 1966). New media for beginning reading have been devised with the aim of regularizing, or at least simplifying, the code. The elimination of alternative pronunciations for the same printed symbol should not only simplify the process of learning to read for the child but should also make discovery methods of learning to read a more practical proposition. Yet progressive teachers who favour heuristic methods are often those who are most reluctant to experiment with new media. It would seem that they have assumed that any attempt to regularize the medium must necessarily be accompanied by a return to formal teaching procedures. Yet this need not be so.

The more regular the new medium, and the more reading materials which are available in it, the more feasible does the possibility of children learning to read by discovery methods become. With an absolutely regular medium and an abundance of reading materials, discovering how to read would fall into the same class as discovering about mathematics and science. While none of the new media mentioned fulfils both criteria, each may be found in different ways to have a certain value for heuristic methods. Reading materials printed in all three colour codes are limited in contrast to i.t.a. with its long list of published reading materials. From the point of regularity, *Words in Colour* is an absolutely regular code; i.t.a., as far as decoding is concerned, approaches regularity very closely; and the remaining two colour codes are better described as partial codes which will help children to pronounce many, but not all, irregular words.*

Alternatively, teachers in progressive schools who do not want to employ a regularized medium for beginning reading should seriously consider the various current means of drawing attention to the regularities of our traditional spelling system.

* See Chapter 8 for a detailed comparison of i.t.a. and three colour codes.

Certain of these approaches, for example, linguistic approaches to reading, do require formal teaching procedures of which such teachers would not approve. On the other hand, certain phonic approaches could fit in very well with the progressive infant teacher's aims regarding active participation and discovery by the children: for example, *Programmed Reading Kit* (Stott 1962) and *Fun With Phonics* (Reis 1962). Other approaches such as *Royal Road Readers* (Daniels and Diack 1957), *Sounds and Words* (Southgate and Havenhand 1959), *Step Up and Read* (Jones 1965), *Six Phonic Workbooks* (Grassam 1966) and *A Remedial Reading Method* (Moxon 1962), while they do require the teacher to adopt the role of instructor for very short periods of time, also provide for plenty of active and individual learning by children.

Yet, progressive infant teachers have been inclined to ignore phonic approaches to reading equally as much as new media, probably because they associated them solely with rigid, formal teaching. Such teachers might do well to consider whether phonic schemes or colour codes, for example, *Words in Colour*, which depend to a certain extent on teacher instruction in the early stages, should be automatically eliminated on that count. It might then be concluded that their use would be more than justified if it led, as it inevitably would, to the child becoming independent earlier. The child whose attention has been drawn to the phonic regularities of our language has been provided with a structured framework which will encourage his interest in words and their spellings, help him to discover and learn the irregularities, and generally make him an independent reader much earlier than the child who is left to discover the regularities and irregularities himself. The child's mastery of reading skills, by enabling him to acquire information from books, will then place him in a much more favourable position for discovery methods of learning in all subjects.

Thus, I am suggesting that teachers in progressive infant schools, who have frequently been those most strongly opposed not only to reading approaches which emphasize the regularities of the code but also to attempts to regularize the code, should be the very ones to show the greatest interest in such developments.

2. A master plan for reading tuition

Efficient reading entails the mastery of many different sub-skills. This is unlikely to occur by chance, without adequate guidance and a certain amount of direct instruction. Accordingly, teachers need to have clear ideas of their aims and detailed plans of exactly what has to be learned and the order and progression of the small steps which will lead to the ultimate goal. In other words, unless a teacher has a master plan children's reading progress will be extremely patchy. Such a plan should include preparatory work before formal reading tuition commences, arrangements for the acquisition of a sight vocabulary of commonly-used words, the development of word attack skills, training in reading with understanding, and reading for different purposes and at different speeds. Arrangement for graded practice and for supplementary reading at progressively more difficult levels need including in this programme, along with some form of checking what has been learned and the keeping of meticulous records. Unless a teacher knows exactly all the minute stages in learning which each child has actually mastered, how can she plan for the next stages?

British educationists are often rather scornful about the formal, detailed plans for reading instruction which exist in American, Canadian and most European schools. We might do better to look carefully at these meticulous plans of what needs to be learned and then, rather than set about *teaching* all of it, attempt so to structure the reading environment that children would be led to discover much of it for themselves.

Only a well-considered master plan, accompanied by accurate diagnosis and meticulous recording, can lead to structuring the learning situation for continuous individual progress. The more informal the classroom regime and the more individualized the reading programme, the more essential does this behind-the-scenes structure become.

3. Selecting and organizing the reading materials

A large proportion of British infant schools now contain extensive collections of miscellaneous books, many of them well produced and illustrated, which children are free to handle at any time. In such an environment, there is no doubt that for many children the motivation to learn to read is strong. Yet, if all or the majority of children are to learn to read, I suggest that this reading environment needs structuring in two ways. First, the selection of books, charts, apparatus and all reading equipment must be the result of a conscientious appraisal undertaken by the teacher in the light of a master plan for reading tuition. Secondly, planned procedures for the use of certain of the reading materials need establishing so that freedom of choice for the child can operate within a framework of graded stages.

The discussion which follows does not apply to those general books such as picture dictionaries, reference books and illustrated story books, which are usually available on display shelves and book corner units in infant classrooms, corridors and entrance halls. It concerns those books and pieces of equipment which have been produced to teach or provide practice in particular stages in learning to read.

Reading books and other reading equipment need to be examined in respect of both content and the required procedures. The content should be so planned as to facilitate child-learning, while procedures for mastering the content should necessitate the child being active, rather than requiring great efforts from the teacher in order to gain small returns from the children. It might be suggested that five minutes teacher-guidance and instruction and fifteen minutes pupil activity is a more appropriate proportion than if these figures are reversed.

The teacher who decides to begin reading with phonic training will find that most phonic reading schemes require quite a large amount of teacher-instruction in the initial stages, although in the later stages minimal teacher-guidance can lead to considerable amounts of learning in the form of pupil-directed activities. If, however, phonic training is introduced after the initial stages of a look-and-say approach, it is possible to find published apparatus, games, equipment and supplementary workbooks which provide active learning situations for children.

If reading begins with a look-and-say method, the first books the child handles should be such that the teacher does not have to put each word into his mouth, and repeat this procedure *ad nauseam* until he has learned the words by rote. If the teacher is to step down from this role of permanent prompter, illustrations, vocabulary control and sentence structure must all be planned to aid the child's independent learning. The illustrations in the books should be so simple, unambiguous and appropriate that the words printed on the page are those which will spring immediately to the child's mind. The structure underlying the build up of words from page to page should be such as to lead the child inevitably and successfully forward. A simple form of sentence structure, used repetitively, will be found more helpful than complicated and varied sentence structures. Many well-known look-and-say reading schemes, and popular supplementary series of books, are deficient in these respects.

Yet look-and-say books can be so structured, with simple words, phrases and stories, accompanied by illustrations which are apposite, that a child can 'read' his first books himself with very little teacher guidance. *What is Little* (Melser 1960), one of the *Read it Yourself Books* is a good example of this, with the text on successive pages reading 'A baby is little', 'a doll is little', and so on. The same is true of *Martin's Toys* (Southgate 1968a), one of the *First Words* series, in which the text under succeeding illustrations reads 'Martin', 'Martin's ball', 'Martin's book', and so on. *This is the Way I Go* (Taylor and Ingleby 1965) and *Methuen Caption Books* (Randell 1966) are additional examples of simple introductory books, so constructed that children can read them with little help from the teacher.

At a slightly more advanced stage, many of the well-known traditional tales containing repetitive phrases, such as 'The Three Little Pigs' and 'The Little Red Hen and The Grain of Wheat', do help the child to read for himself. So too do books such as the *Reading with Rhythm* books (Taylor and Ingleby 1961), *Mouse Books* (Piers 1966) and *Stories for Me* (Ryder 1957) and *Spring-board Readers* (Mail 1968). Most of these books also employ the helpful technique of presenting meaningful phrases as separate lines of print. They are all simple stories which by means of phrasing, rhythm and repetition are so designed that very little teacher guidance is required. The *Oxford Colour Readers* (Carver and Stowasser 1963) is a particularly good example of a reading scheme for older retarded pupils which is planned in such a way as to help the child to help himself.

The selection of equipment, supposedly designed to help children to read, requires particular caution, as it can frequently prove no more than a time-filler. One should consider exactly what the child will be learning by playing a game or using a piece of apparatus—whether the apparatus has been designed to guide the child towards a particular discovery, to reinforce his learning, or to provide him with practice in a newly acquired skill. Different clues and self-checking devices are required at different stages. For instance, if the child is being guided to recognize the initial sounds of words, by matching two pieces of card, one bearing the letter *e* and the other the picture of an egg, a simple clue, such as a background colour or a jig-saw shape, might help him to do so with little chance of failure. At the same time, the teacher needs to be aware that the child is likely to use the minimum clue necessary to achieve success. If he can match a red colour to a red colour or fit a sticking-out curve into an inward bending curve, he will not necessarily note that the printed symbol *e* relates to the initial sound of the word 'egg'. After some practice at this particular stage, his knowledge of initial letter sounds could only be checked by removing extraneous clues from the front of the pieces of card, and replacing them by self-checking devices on the back.

This raises the important point of the distinction between clues and self-checking devices. Clues are clearly visible and help the child to make the correct moves. The clues themselves should be sufficiently simple for the child to understand them on his own; for example, indistinguishable colours, or similarly shaped jig-saw pieces which require the teacher's aid, defeat their own object. Clues cannot be considered as real self-checking devices, because they do not necessarily indicate to the teacher whether or not the child has mastered the reading skill which the apparatus was designed to help him to learn. Thus clues should be used solely in the preliminary stage of learning any skill. Real self-checking devices only come into effect *after* the child has completed the operation. They should indicate that the child has mastered the relevant skill *without* extraneous clues. A teacher would be wise to hesitate before purchasing or using reading games and apparatus which lack true self-checking devices, unless she can see ways in which such devices can be added. Otherwise, children will spend a few brief minutes carrying out the activity and long periods waiting for the teacher to check what they have done.

With all equipment and apparatus, as with books, the teacher needs to consider the ratio of her instruction time to the pupil's learning time. Apparatus and games which require lengthy or complicated instructions are rarely worthwhile, unless the technique being mastered is one which can be repeatedly utilized for other learning. The game of Bingo or Lotto, for instance, is well worth teaching as it can be played over and over again for practising different skills.

It should also be noted that many sets of apparatus for beginning reading, relating to both sight words and phonically regular words, concentrate almost exclusively on nouns. Yet, McNally and Murray (1962) who list 200 'key' words which account for 'half to three-quarters of the running words occurring in everyday reading matter', note that only 21 of these are nouns. Clearly children's early reading progress will be facilitated if the sight of these 200 key words evokes automatic responses from them. In fact, much of the time which children spend playing with ill-designed pieces of apparatus, relating to nouns they are unlikely to encounter in their reading books, could be much more profitably spent in activities designed to aid their instant recognition of the most common, and often irregular, words in our language. This need not be done by drilled instruction, although, as children are unlikely to discover how to read these irregular words for themselves, the teacher may at first need to take a leading role in group games to ensure superficial mastery of the words. Perfect mastery can then be accomplished by means of activities and games undertaken by groups of children or individual children without the teacher's help. McNally and Murray (1962) in *Key Words to Literacy* suggest a few games for learning 'key words'. Galt publish games entitled *Key Words Self-Teaching Cards* consisting mainly of nouns, and also *Basic Words Lotto* and *Key Words Lotto* containing a proportion of words other than nouns. Many practising teachers have also developed their own apparatus and games designed to aid children's mastery of these words. It is a pity that their ideas are not more publicized.

Yet the selection of appropriate reading materials is only part of the plan for structuring the reading environment towards individualized child-learning. My second suggestion was that the skilful pre-organization by the teacher of a considerable proportion of the available reading materials was necessary before children's free choice became operative. As far as reading games and apparatus are concerned, infant teachers usually accept that children should use them in a particular sequence, rather than in random order which would nullify their graded levels of difficulty. Yet, in certain infant classes this principle is not accepted for books.

I believe we need to develop a form of procedure half-way between that of children's unrestricted access to a miscellaneous collection of books, and complete reliance on a basic reading scheme under the teacher's direct control. Once motivation to learn to read is aroused, not only are small amounts of instruction valuable but graded practice is also necessary. This can best be arranged by ensuring that, at every stage, a child can be guided to choose books and equipment from a selection appropriate to his level of attainment. Both the miscellaneous collection and the graded collection of books are necessary. For the latter, the teacher needs to select certain simple books at different levels, which should be so arranged, on different shelves or marked with distinctive bindings, that every child can always know where to find something of interest which both he and his teacher realize he will be able to read with a fair degree of success.

Many of the books already mentioned can be selected to fulfil this purpose. So can the supplementary books of many look-and-say reading schemes, for example *McKee Platform Readers* (Castley *et al.* 1958–61), *Janet and John Supplementary Books* (O'Donnell and Munro 1951), and also the supplementary books of certain phonic approaches, for example *Gay Way Red Stories*, etc. (Boyce 1959), *Royal Road Miniatures, Royal Road First and Second Companion Books*, and *Sounds and Words Stories* (Southgate 1967). The child who has read the preceding basic book and is able to recognize the appropriate sight words or grasp the relevant phonic rules, as the case may be, can be left free to choose his own supplementary book and to read it by himself. The phonic supplementary books can also prove valuable for the child who has been reading a look-and-say scheme and whose teacher has introduced incidental phonic words, providing the child is given access to them at the appropriate stages. Both look-and-say and phonic supplementary books, wisely chosen and introduced as part of a plan of graded practice, provide perfect opportunities for individual choice within a structured framework. Yet how often one sees these very books being used in two opposing, and equally inappropriate, ways.

The 'progressive' teacher often places on display shelves simple supplementary books from many schemes for children's free choice. Then children, not fully prepared for them, pick up these books at random and, finding them too difficult, quickly discard them. We should realize that although supplementary books from different look-and-say reading schemes may look of equivalent simplicity this is not so. The overlap of words between one scheme and another is not nearly as great as one might imagine. In contrast, the more formal teacher often uses a different procedure. She insists on 'hearing' the child read all the supplementary books in a reading scheme. What a waste of opportunity for individual choice and private reading practice!

Neither of these extreme forms of procedure seems to me to be entirely successful. To have every step of reading tuition dominated by the teacher can crush the eagerness of the young child, deprive him of the pleasure of freedom of choice and sap his initiative. On the other hand, complete freedom for the child to try to read materials which the teacher knows to be too difficult for him is merely providing him with a frustrating situation. I believe that subtle arrangements made by the teacher, to ensure the child's inevitable success with the books he chooses to read or the reading games which he plays, would represent the most practical form of freedom likely to ensure individual learning. Accordingly, although the selection of reading books and equipment to form graded collections at different levels of difficulty is not an easy task, I am certain that it is important for us to devote more attention to it.

IV SUMMING UP

There are many advantages to be gained when the emphasis in beginning reading is on pupil-learning rather than on teacher-instruction. Yet the creation of a school environment designed to promote motivated, individualized learning should not lead to the conclusion that all instruction should be taboo. In fact, I am certain that the ideas now being developed in our 'progressive' primary schools will soon become discredited if they are accompanied by an acceptance of the idea that it is no part of the role of a teacher to teach.

The freer the school environment, from the child's point of view, the more carefully should the teacher have structured it, particularly with regard to learning to read. There are three main reasons for this conclusion. First, English is not a regular language and therefore does not lend itself so easily to discovery methods of learning as do mathematics and science. Secondly, as heuristic methods of learning can only be fully developed when facility in reading and writing has been acquired, the creation of some structure in the process of learning to read and write becomes even more important in progressive schools. Thirdly, the position of changing staffs in primary schools strengthens the need for a certain amount of structure in reading tuition.

Three broad ways of structuring the reading environment have been suggested. First, systems of regularizing the written code or of drawing attention to the existing rules should be stringently examined rather than being discarded out of hand as inappropriate, particularly for progressive schools. Secondly, in both formal and informal schools, every teacher requires a master plan for reading tuition, the latter probably having even more need of it than the former. Thirdly, all reading materials should be selected in the light of how they will encourage children to help themselves. Procedures for the use of these reading materials should be so planned that children's freedom of choice will operate within a framework of graded stages.

4 Early Reading

A paper presented at the Third Annual Conference of the United Kingdom Reading Association, Cambridge, July 1966; and later published in Browne, A. L. (ed.) 1967 READING CURRENT RESEARCH AND PRACTICE

I   INTRODUCTION

As the fourth and final speaker invited to prepare a contribution in advance for this teach-in on early reading, the writing of the usual kind of paper to be read to you appeared inappropriate. It occurred to me that by the time a teach-in had continued all day, it was more than likely that anything which I had written in advance would already have been discussed by one or more of the preceding participants. Moreover, as the final contributor I considered that I should attempt to sum up, albeit beforehand, some of the contrasting views likely to have been expressed during the course of the day.

Accordingly, I have assembled a number of the points which are usually made both for and against early reading. These I have tried to systematize and enumerate under two main headings: first, the arguments which are usually brought forward against early reading, and secondly, points which I think could well be made in reply to these arguments. The presentation of these opposing points of view affords me the opportunity to list my own conclusions on this subject. Thus my contribution to this teach-in, rather than being in the form of a piece of prose, consists of a collection of points presented in note form within a particular framework.

II   ARGUMENTS AGAINST EARLY READING

Arguments against 'early reading', whatever that may be taken to mean, may be divided into two main categories. The first category supports the belief that children cannot learn to read at an early age because the task is too difficult for them. The second group of arguments against early reading concludes that, even if children could do so, they should not.

A.   *Children cannot*

The most common arguments brought forward by people who state that children cannot learn to read at a very early age may be summarized as follows.

1.   Children are not ready to begin to read until they have a Mental Age of six and a half.
2.   Young children are not able to make fine visual discriminations.
3.   Young children are not able to make fine auditory discriminations.
4.   When some children first attend school their speech is not sufficiently fluent for them to be ready to begin to read.
5.   In short, the task of learning to read is too difficult for many children when they first start school.
6.   Because the task is too difficult for young children, attempts to teach them to read at an early age must necessarily result in pressure being placed on them.
7.   If young children are 'pushed' into reading and made to work, they may be unhappy.
8.   Because the task is too difficult many children will fail.

B.   *Even if children can—they should not*

The arguments of those who believe that, even if children are able to learn to read at an early age, they should not be encouraged to do so, usually run along the following lines.

1.   Time devoted to the teaching of reading is time snatched

from more important activities: for example, play, creative activities and exploration of the environment.

2. If we left the teaching of reading until later (seven or some specified age), it would come naturally and more easily.

3. Even if children are taught to read at an earlier age, they will be no further forward at eleven (or some specified age).

4. Attempts should not be made to teach children to read earlier because many of them will fail.

C. *The failing child*

The thought of the failing child is inherent in both the foregoing main lines of argument. On all sides there emerges a real concern about children who are expected to learn to read, whom teachers try to teach to read, who nevertheless fail to learn to read and who may thus develop adverse attitudes to reading. This sort of argument, put forward by both sets of opponents of early reading, is the one which merits our most serious consideration.

III REPLIES TO THE ARGUMENTS AGAINST EARLY READING

A. *Children can*

1. There is no doubt about it that many children can, and do, begin to read at a very early age. A mass of evidence is accumulating on this score and it is important to notice that this evidence does not relate merely to bright children. A few examples of such evidence may be cited.

a. Diack (1963) gives details of some children as young as two years old being able to recognize letters and words.

b. Lynn (1963) lists a number of children with Chronological Ages of less than three and Mental Ages of less than three and a half successfully identifying whole words.

c. Glynn (1964) in her book *Teach Your Child to Read*, although in no way advocating that parents should 'push' their children into early reading, does show mothers '. . . some of the ways in which you can, without forcing his pace, help your child to be busy about reading, even before he goes to school . . .'

d. Some parents now report that their pre-school children are learning to read, using the early books of *Key Words Reading Scheme* (Murray 1964).

e. Downing (1963), Harrison (1964), Southgate (1963) and others have given examples of many four-year-olds learning to read with i.t.a.

f. Doman (1965), who worked with a team of specialists on brain-injured children in the U.S.A., says, 'When the team had seen many brain-injured children read, and read well, at three years of age and younger, it became obvious that something was wrong with what was happening to normal children.' He further states that 'Tiny children *want* to learn to read, *can* learn to read, *are* learning to read and *should* learn to read.'

g. Moore (1963) describes children aged between two and a half years and six years, in the U.S.A., learning to read and write by means of an electric 'talking' typewriter. Not all these children are what he describes as 'ultra-rapid learners'; some are 'ultra-slow learners'.

2. The concept of a Mental Age of six and a half being the 'minimum for probable success' in reading, as put forward by Morphett and Washburne (1931), while being helpful in drawing attention to some of the problems of slower children has, because of the manner in which it was taken up by later writers, done untold harm to the cause of reading. The results have been that some teachers and other educators have assumed that no one should begin to do anything about reading until children are six and a half years of age and that, even then, half the age-group are not sufficiently mature to begin reading. Sanderson, Lynn and Downing, in a symposium entitled 'Reading Readiness' in *Educational Research* (1963), provide an interesting re-examination of this question. The growth of the concept of the importance of a mental age of six and a half has tended to encourage the idea that reading readiness is a stage to be waited for and not something for which training programmes can be planned. Yet, at the same time, many infant teachers have been successfully helping children

whose Mental Ages were less than six and a half years to learn to read.

3.   The belief that young children cannot make fine visual discriminations is rapidly being exploded. Diack and Lynn both give examples of children from two to five years being able to do so, after a little practice. Some recent unpublished research of my own showed that many children less than five years old, who had not begun to read, could make fine visual discriminations between words of similar appearance. For example, one child of four years was able to discriminate between the words 'boot' and 'boat' (although he could not read these words) by the fact that one 'had an extra stick—there', as he said, pointing to the letter *a* in 'boat'. Furthermore, in this research, the investigators, who were making every effort not to teach, all reported on the enormous increase in the children's ability to make fine visual discriminations during the course of three or four short experimental sessions.

4.   Exactly the same can be said about young children's ability to make fine auditory discrimination. To be able to do so is not merely an aspect of normal maturation. It can be helped immensely by graded practice, in the form of various games, as many infant teachers have already discovered.

5.   I would agree with those who state that at the stage when they enter school some children's speech is so inadequate that it would be inappropriate for them to try to learn to read. Nevertheless, while a certain fluency in speech is desirable before reading begins, one should not forget that reading readiness training is a great aid to an improvement in the spoken language. Furthermore, reading instruction and reading practice can increase the child's vocabulary, not merely of the words which he understands but also of those he uses in both written and spoken expression.

6.   To those who believe that the task of learning to read is a complicated one which is too difficult for many children at the stage when they first start school, one must suggest that it is a mistake to assume that *all* ways of learning to read are too difficult. It has always been accepted that exceptionally able teachers were able to use methods which greatly simplified the learning process for the child. This is now being carried further by those

interested in programmed learning. The use of various systems of simplified spelling has, in the past and more recently in the case of i.t.a., been shown to make the process easier. Modern teaching aids including tape-recorders, typewriters (electric and otherwise), television, films and various teaching machines may all contribute to a simplification of the process of learning to read. And all such simplification will tend to make earlier reading possible.

7.   With those who oppose early reading on the grounds that children may be asked to work and that this will be bad for them and make them unhappy, I have no patience whatsoever. Why should we assume that an interesting task is hard work which young children will wish to avoid and that to ask them to do it will cause them suffering? Most young children do not differentiate between work and play. They love to 'work hard' at something in which they are interested and with which they can achieve a measure of success. Most of the authors mentioned earlier tell of young children's joy, pride and satisfaction in early reading.

B.   *Children should*

I am inclined to regard the majority of the arguments put forward by those who say that even if children can begin to read earlier, they should not do so, as nonsense. If children want to learn to read, if they are interested in doing so and if they can do so, I believe we should not discourage them. Of the four usual arguments put forward by opponents of early reading, I shall make a brief reply to the first three and add a number of further reasons why I think children should learn to read as early as possible. (The fourth argument of opponents of early reading, regarding failing children, will be dealt with separately later.)

1.   Some educationists hold that the time devoted by young children to learning to read is time that would be better devoted to other pursuits. I disagree entirely with this line of thought for two reasons.

a.   Surely language in its spoken, written and printed forms, is just as much part of the child's environment as water, clay, paint, paste and paper. I am at a loss to understand why we should be expected to commend children's explorations of these aspects of their environment, but not their interest in, and exploration of, printed and written words and letters which form an equally important and interesting aspect of their environment. Why is it so horrifying to some teachers if we encourage a child when he shows signs of being interested in words? The child who can differentiate and identify different makes of cars, trains, aeroplanes, or flowers is applauded by all of us. We say that he is showing initiative and we must encourage him to explore this interesting world around him. Yet clearly some people think it more valuable for the young child to delve into archaeology, ornithology or any other field of study, than that of the printed word.

b.   Secondly, those who deplore time spent on early reading rarely pause to consider the shortness of the actual time which would be devoted to it. Most of the teaching and learning in the early stages is incidental; speaking, as well as writing and reading a few words go on alongside, and are intermingled with, all the other activities of the infant school. Direct instruction, if indeed it takes place at all, is unlikely to last for more than a few minutes. Practice in recognizing sentences, words, or letters is usually in the form of games, and I am afraid that I am not convinced that it is more profitable, or indeed more enjoyable, for young children to indulge in games and activities concerned with, say, number concepts than in similar activities concerned with words or letters.

2.   The second argument produced by the opponents of early reading is that reading will come naturally if it is left until later —but they do not often say how much later. I consider this argument to be fallacious, and I am certain that those of you who have had to deal with non-readers in junior and secondary modern classes will support me in this. Learning to read is not a feature of physical maturation, as for example walking which occurs naturally in nearly all children. It is a complex skill and most children need a good deal of help and guidance if they are to acquire it. Certainly some of our brighter children learn to read

very easily, apparently almost unaided, but with others reading might never come naturally. There are some children who might never be motivated to read unless someone inspired them to do so or actually got them started. They would never know that they would enjoy it until they had commenced, in the same way as a child does not know how much pleasure he will gain from eating certain foods until some adult has encouraged him to taste them.

3.   The third argument against early reading generally takes the line that there is no point in children learning to read at an early age as they will be no better readers anyway by the time they reach, for example, the age of ten or eleven. Two points may be made in reply to this argument.

a.   Even if children who learn to read at an early age are not any further advanced in their reading ability at eleven, this does not represent a valid reason for decrying early reading. Such an argument assumes that each stage of development in the child is only important because of what it leads to. Clearly the end product in education is important, but I should like to think that each stage on the way to the end product is also of value for its own sake. Accordingly, I would suggest that if reading at five or earlier gives the child pleasure and satisfaction, widens his horizons, enriches his environment, or produces any other benefits, this is a fact which merits great value being attached to it, even if early reading is not followed by better performance at a later age.

b.   If children who learn to read at, say, five are no further advanced in reading ability at eleven than if they had commenced two years later, it may well be because we, as teachers, have not yet learned to help children to develop and utilize this skill to the full. There is a tendency for teachers of junior classes to assume that if children are reading fluently at the level of a Reading Age of seven or eight, that instruction in the skill of reading is completed and that all the child requires is practice, mainly in silent reading. If children begin to learn to read earlier, as I am certain they will, we must be prepared to devote more time to perfecting children's study skills in reading, as well as training them to utilize all their reading skills to the utmost extent.

The following are some of the additional reasons why I consider that children should be encouraged to learn to read as soon as they can happily do so.

4. Many children *want* to learn to read and write. We are all familiar with the old story of the child who came home disappointed after his first day at school because he had not learned to read. Most children want to imitate grown-ups in all sorts of ways. If a child wants to garden or use woodwork tools, we offer him every assistance. We are amused and pleased by his efforts to imitate Daddy. We provide him with real tools and real wood. The same is true of the little girl who wishes to cook. We do not say to her nowadays, 'Cooking is too hard for you; when you are a bigger girl you'll be able to learn.' Certain infant schools now provide not only woodwork benches and tools but also cooking stoves so that young children can enjoy baking real cakes. Yet if the child wants to read real books or write real words, there are some educationists who throw up their hands in horror because the five-year-old is too young to read! I feel that however young the child, if he desires to explore this aspect of his environment, if he wishes to imitate adults by reading and writing, it is the duty of the adults concerned to devise the simplest possible means for initiating him into this activity.

5. As well as most children themselves wanting to learn to read, most parents also want their children to read. This is partly because it is the one tangible measure that parents have of their children's progress in schools. When parents visit infant schools this is the question they most often ask teachers. I am not suggesting that teachers should always react to pressure from parents in this way. Yet there is a case for appreciating that many parents whose children are unable to read by the age of seven feel worried about it. Such anxiety can easily rub off on the children and create an atmosphere unfavourable to learning. Early reading can help to avoid this detrimental aspect of the situation, although I am aware that there could be dangers in parents endeavouring to bring pressure on teachers regarding children who are unable to read at an early age.

6. One great advantage of early reading and writing is that it provides children with an additional means of self-expression.

One only needs to read some of the examples of young children's free writing in *The Excitement of Writing* (Clegg 1964) to appreciate this. Many publications referring to the use of i.t.a. have also given examples of young children expressing themselves in writing. One recent example I came across springs to mind. I visited a school in a very poor area, on a day of pouring rain in June. The area surrounding the school held very little of beauty but there were a few flowering cherry trees in blossom in some of the gardens. A rather pathetic-looking little boy, just under six, had written something like this in his diary. (The original was in i.t.a. and was not punctuated.)

'It is raining today and I am sad. We cannot go out to play because it is raining so hard. But I guess the blossoms like the rain. They are so lovely that I could just kiss them.'

This piece of prose, which starts off by relating facts and how they affect the child personally, then goes on to reveal a marvellous experience of aesthetic appreciation. The boy was not very intelligent and rather inarticulate. If he had not acquired some fluency in reading and writing by this stage, it could well have been that this particular experience of appreciation of beauty would never have found expression.

7. Early reading and writing not only gives children an additional mode of expression but also provides them with a further means of communication. If they can read books, then the authors can communicate directly with the children. If children can read handwritten notes and letters, distant relatives and friends can communicate directly with them, as can the adults and children nearby. Once they can write, there is no barrier to the child communicating in this way with whomever he wishes, in any part of the world. I saw an amusing instance of this aspect of communicating recently. As the five-year-olds were leaving an infant school at the end of the afternoon, the headmistress noticed that Kevin was clutching a large folded piece of drawing paper. She asked him what it was and Kevin replied that it was a note for his Mummy. As it did not look like the kind of letter his teacher would have sent to a parent, the headmistress asked if she could look at it. Inside was a message from Kevin's friend, John, to Kevin's mother. It read: 'Please tell your Kevin to stop fighting

or you will put him to bed.' (The spelling has been corrected.) John had not told Kevin what was in the note and Kevin, being rather dull, had not asked! One may deplore or be amused by the tale-telling aspect of this incident yet one must accept that, in order to fulfil a need which he felt, this young child was utilizing a newly acquired means of communication with an adult.

8. The foregoing story leads easily to the next advantage of early reading and writing. Children who have made a beginning in reading and writing are thereby given independence and an aid to the development of initiative. John, when he wrote his note, demonstrated both these qualities. Teachers do not need me to give them further examples of how children who have achieved even a simple level of these two skills soon begin to depend less on the teacher and more on themselves.

9. My next point is related to the probable staffing position in infant schools in the foreseeable future. It seems highly likely that large classes and changing staffs are going to be with us for a considerable number of years. The hardships experienced by both children and teachers in these difficult circumstances can be mitigated somewhat by children's independence when they have mastered even the initial stages of the skills of reading and writing.

10. Finally, the growing trend in primary education is towards heuristic methods. While it is true that discovery methods can be, and are being, utilized in many different ways by children who cannot read and write, yet it must be accepted that the inability to employ either skill will necessarily prove a limiting factor. The child who can read and write, and is consequently able to consult books on the subjects which currently interest him, will be able to progress much further with discovery methods on individual lines than the child who must rely only on the evidence of his own senses supplemented by verbal enquiries to his teacher.

C. *Need children fail?*

Both the people who say that children cannot learn to read and those who say that even if children can, they should not, are concerned with the thought that early reading will increase the

proportion of reading failures. Those of us who in certain circumstances are not opposed to early reading are equally concerned
about this problem. I am certain that we all ask ourselves if children need to fail or, even more important, if they need feel that
they have failed. In this connection the following points are
relevant.

1. When a child feels that he has failed to learn to read, his
feelings are more often related to what he thinks parents and
teachers expect of him than to his own expectations. Consequently both parents and teachers must be on their guard against
setting aims and standards which the child may not be able to
reach.
2. The climate of expectation in a school is extremely important. For example, a school which gives very high priority to
teaching children to read may well teach more children to read
than a school which has more broadly based aims; yet it is possible
that this very strong emphasis on reading may cause the few children who fail to learn to read in the first school to experience
greater feelings of failure than do the non-readers in the second
school.
3. I am not certain that delaying the beginning of reading will
necessarily either avert or reduce the problem of children failing.
It is not easy to draw comparisons of reading results between
different countries in which children begin school at different ages.
However, there does not appear to be a smaller percentage of
retardation in the U.S.A., or in some European countries where
children start school later, than in Great Britain. In fact there is
some evidence to the contrary, for example:

a. Doman (1965) suggests that the later we leave reading, the
more difficult it becomes, but he does not give any concrete
evidence about this;
b. Taylor's (1950) experiments suggest that early teaching of
reading increases performance;
c. Anderson's (1964) study, comparing American, Scottish and
English children, has similar results.

4. As teachers, I think we must accept that at whatever age

children begin to learn to read and whatever means we use to help them, not all children will be successful, or not all will be equally successful. This will be true even when we are much more skilled than we are at present in preparing for and assessing reading readiness, in simplifying the task, in utilizing motivation, in diagnosing difficulties and in all the many other factors which contribute to our ability to help children to learn to read. If we accept that not all children will be equally successful, it is particularly important that the children themselves should accept differences in reading skills as coming within the normal range of differences. Most young children accept that some of them are tall and some short, that some are better at painting than others, and some are good at kicking a ball while others are not so good. We need to create an atmosphere in which differences in reading ability are no more emotionally toned than differences in hair colouring.

5.   The feeling of failure in children can be substantially reduced by a release of tension and anxiety about reading in both teachers and parents. Teachers need to truly accept a wide range of individual differences in children and hence a wide range of different beginning ages. At present we pay lip-service to individual differences in children, while at the same time trying to make a beginning with reading with most children at about the age of five and a half.

6.   Differences between children's performances are less noticeable in the informal classroom than the formal one. Similarly, reading abilities are not so easily comparable within classes comprising children of different ages, in vertically grouped classes, or in classes in small rural schools, for instance, as they are in classes in which children are all the same age. Within a mixed age-group a child is much less likely to realize that he is a late starter or a slow learner and consequently less likely to feel himself a failure.

7.   It is also probable that both children and their parents would be less conscious of failure if the children within a class were using a wide variety of reading books rather than all using one basic reading scheme.

8.   While accepting that not all children will be ready to begin

to read at the same time, nevertheless I consider it fatal just to wait for reading readiness to appear as if by magic. There is much that we can do to help children to be ready for reading. We need to be more highly qualified ourselves in the skills of reading. Then we could:

a.   arrange for much more spoken communication;
b.   provide more practice in visual and auditory discrimination;
c.   and make more detailed plans for encouraging children's interests in books, and in reading and writing.

By these means we could ensure that the process of working towards reading readiness would constitute a dynamic programme for the slower child, which would satisfy him and make him conscious of his own progress, while at the same time carrying him forward to the point at which he was ready for a more formal reading programme.

9.   When a child has actually begun to read, we need to be specialists who can give him specific guidance and instruction which will help him to avoid or overcome the 'sticking points'. Such skilled help would go a long way beyond merely 'hearing him read' and prompting him when he fails.

10.   We need always to be willing to explore new ways of simplifying the task, as simplification must necessarily result in fewer failures. However successful we feel we have been in teaching children to read in certain ways, we should still look with open minds at further ideas which might help children to read more easily.

IV   CONCLUSIONS

1.   We need to accept a far greater range of ages for beginning reading than we do at present. This implies that many children should begin earlier, as well as that some should start much later.

2.   Many young children can and do begin to read very happily. I have long suspected that we seriously underestimate children. In the right situations many more may enjoy reading at an early age than at present.

3. There is every reason why children who can begin early should do so. Their own enjoyment and pride, the extension of their interests, the growth of their independence and initiative and the fact that they will have another medium of communication, all support this view. Conditions in present-day schools, as well as modern heuristic methods, reinforce the conclusion that we should encourage children to read and write as soon as they are able to do so.

4. We should accept that a few children may not be ready to begin formal reading even by the time they leave the infant school. We need to be able to recognize such children at an early stage so that we may arrange for them a developmental programme of pre-reading experiences which will form a firm basis for later reading, while at the same time providing them with the satisfaction of perceiving their own progress.

5. We need to be continually aiming to simplify the task of learning to read and write. New media, in the form of simplified alphabets, colour codes or other ideas, new teaching methods, as well as new reading materials and teaching aids, should all be explored with this end in view.

Part Two *New media for beginning reading*

5 Augmented Roman Alphabet Experiment: an Outsider's Report

An article published in EDUCATIONAL REVIEW, *Vol. 16, No. 1, pp. 32–41, November 1963.*

I INTRODUCTION

The current British experiment[1] into the use of the Augmented Roman Alphabet (A.R.),* as a means of teaching the early stages of reading, began in September 1961. (See: Pitman 1961, Downing 1962a and 1962b, and Gardner 1962.) During the course of this experiment many reports will doubtless be issued by those who are responsible for mounting it, as well as by teachers who are taking part in it. It is equally certain that a great number of teachers and educators will be awaiting with interest the results of the experiment. Yet those who are not actually engaged in experimenting with a new approach to teaching frequently have a measure of scepticism regarding claims of remarkable results which may be made by obviously enthusiastic participants in an experiment. In these circumstances, an account from an independent observer may have some value.

This account concerns one experimental class in the current A.R. experiment and it is probably relevant to relate how I came to be in the privileged position of an independent observer of the work in this class. When it was announced that a certain local education authority in the north of England was to take part in this experiment, I told the Director of Education of my interest in the early stages of learning to read and asked permission to

---

* Later renamed the Initial Teaching Alphabet (i.t.a.).

observe the experiment. My request was granted and I was given complete freedom to go into any experimental school within the local authority at any time, as well as to attend meetings of teachers concerned in the experiment. The class referred to in this report is one which I have visited regularly and informally from the inception of the experiment. The testing mentioned in this report was not carried out at the instigation of anyone concerned with the experiment, but arose as a result of my observations of the progress being made by the children. All testing was carried out by myself, with no other adult in the room.

II   THE FIRST THREE TERMS

This particular infant school is situated in the centre of a large council housing estate from which all its children are drawn. The headmistress of the school described herself as originally 'a grudging participant' in the experiment, in that she was not anxious to commit children to being taught by an approach which was not yet proven. As it happens, the children in this area start school at the beginning of the school year in which they will reach their fifth birthday. In September 1961 the 68 new entrants to the school were divided between two classes, according to age: 38 children aged 5 years 0 months to 4 years 5 months formed the older class of new entrants, while the younger class consisted of 30 children aged 4 years 5 months to 4 years 0 months. It was the younger class which was committeed to the A.R. experiment. The headmistress had finally agreed to allow these very young children to participate in the experiment because, as she said, four year olds are not usually given formal training in reading, and thus if the experiment proved abortive there would still be time for the children to begin to learn to read by more orthodox means at the age of five.

During the autumn term of 1961, my visits to the class and talks with the teacher and the children led me to conclude that this was a group of four year olds of average intelligence who were following the normal school routine one would expect for children of their age. It was clear that there was no pressure whatsoever towards learning to read and write. Pictures and objects in the room were labelled in A.R., instead of orthodox print. The book corner contained fewer books than in most infant classrooms because of the paucity of books printed in A.R. at that time. Apart from these two differences one could have been in any ordinary reception class. At the beginning of the term, wall charts and a few of the books in the *Janet and John* (O'Donnell and Munro 1949) reading scheme, printed in A.R., had arrived in the school, but the supplementary books for the scheme were not then available. Neither the headteacher nor the class teacher were perturbed about the lack of reading books because, as they indicated, they were not expecting to do any formal teaching of reading during this first term nor probably, for some children, during the whole of their first year.

During the spring term 1962, it became apparent that many of the quicker children in the class were making very rapid strides with reading. They were progressing steadily through the reading scheme. In addition, they were not only handling but actually reading many books from the book corner. Most of the slower children in the class, who were not judged ready to begin the reading scheme, were showing a much greater interest in books than usual. The reactions of the entire class to the reading situation were what one might have expected from children a year or more older than themselves.

Towards the end of the summer term 1962, reading progress in the class was as follows. Ten children had read as far as *Janet and John Book 4*, including the appropriate supplementary books. They had also read a large number of book-corner books printed in A.R. It was estimated that a few of the better readers had read something like two hundred books each. Admittedly, some of the two hundred were very simple books with only a sentence or two per page, but others contained a great deal of print; two examples are *Little Black Sambo* and *Henry the Green Engine*.

Twelve children, who might be termed 'the middle group', were halfway through *Janet and John Book 3*, having completed the preceding basic readers and supplementary books in the scheme. They had also read varying numbers of books from the book corner.

Of the remaining eight children, six had read *Janet and John Book 1* and the relevant supplementary books and were engaged on reading the basic *Book 2*. These six children knew the sounds of the 43 [2] characters in A.R. and could blend them into words, although they were not very fluent. Only two children in the class had made less progress; they could recognize a few words by sight and knew the sounds of some of the characters.

A note on the children's writing would seem apposite at this point. During the first term the children had not been encouraged to do any writing, as the headmistress was doubtful of the value of training children to write an alphabet which they would later need to forget. During the second term, some children began to write sentences and 'stories' spontaneously. By the third term, a great deal of free writing was being done. Because of the regularity of A.R. spelling the children experienced no difficulty in making a good approximation to the correct (A.R.) spelling of any word they wanted to write. They thus acquired no adverse attitude towards the normal difficulties of spelling, and the result was a greater volume and a higher standard of free writing than the school had ever experienced with a class of this age.

Two other interesting developments occurred during the children's third term in school. First, many children became so absorbed in reading books that they had literally to be driven into the playground at playtime and after lunch, even on fine sunny days. In fact, the headmistress became rather worried about such young children wanting to spend so much time with books. Secondly, it was discovered that one or two children had by accident found themselves able to read orthodox script. Books in traditional print had been deliberately kept from them at school and at home. There was no intention on the part of the school to encourage these children to make the transfer from A.R. to orthodox print until a much later stage. Indeed, all sorts of plans had been made as to how children could be taught to make the transfer. Yet here were one or two children, barely five years old, who by chance had obtained library books in traditional print from older brothers and sisters or from the town library, and who could read them with no apparent difficulty. Two of the books in question were *Black Beauty* and *Treasure Island*.

One of the vital questions regarding learning to read by means of A.R. lies in the problem of the transfer from A.R. to orthodox print. Until the children have made this transfer and can be tested in the normal medium of traditional print, results of success with A.R. are bound to be considered with caution, even by those who do not entirely discount them. For instance, the use of 'transliterated' copies of well-known standardized Graded Word Reading Tests, with children who can read A.R., would appear to be of little or no value. Once a child can recognize and sound the 43 characters of A.R. and has learned to blend these sounds together to make words, it is theoretically possible for him to read any word in A.R., regardless of how difficult the word may be considered in normal print. A child of any age, who had acquired these techniques in Augmented Roman, might well be able to pronounce the words in the bottom line of print on one of the well-known Graded Word Reading Tests, if it had been 'transliterated' into A.R. To convert such a performance into a reading age of fifteen years or more would obviously be meaningless.

Thus the only results which could begin to offer any valid comparison between learning to read using A.R. as opposed to the normal alphabet would be results obtained from standardized tests in traditional print. Such tests will no doubt be used in the experiment, when children have officially made the transfer in school from books using A.R. to books using traditional script, and after they have attained familiarity and fluency in the new medium. It was not expected that this stage would be reached by average children until they were seven or seven and a half years old. However, knowing that a number of the young children in this particular class had made the transfer to orthodox print on their own and with apparent ease, it seemed worth-while to let them attempt a simple standardized reading test in traditional print.

The test selected was *Southgate Group Reading Test One— Word Selection Test* (Southgate 1959) in which the test papers were likely to appeal to young children because they contained many pictures. The test had been standardized on six-year-old children and, although it had been established that an occasional very bright child of five could manage it, the test was not recommended for general use with five-year-olds. Indeed, before encountering the children in the present class, I should have been horrified at the thought of this test being used with children barely five years old.

In view of the results obtained, it is important to appreciate the difficulties under which these children were labouring in undertaking a group reading test. They were taken in small groups into a classroom other than their own. They were seated at individual tables, well spaced out from each other and all facing the front of the room; a very different situation from their usual habit of sitting clustered round tables in small companionable groups. Furthermore they were debarred from looking at their neighbours' papers to see what had been done and to give or obtain help from each other as they normally did. They were also discouraged from talking about what they were doing. In fact, it was an entirely different social situation from that found in the normal classroom. The children were then asked to carry out definite instructions in a specified manner; for example, 'Point to the first word in the first box.' The words on the test papers were somewhat smaller than most of the print they had encountered in their reading books. Finally, the words were printed in traditional script, although I did not comment on this fact.

Despite all these drawbacks and the fact that only two or three of the children had previously attempted to read traditional script, all the children appeared to enjoy trying to play these so-called games. The better readers in the class were allowed to go on attempting items until I considered they had reached their limit. No child was allowed to go on straining to do something which was clearly too difficult for him, yet each child was led to believe that he had made a successful attempt. Even the slowest reader in the class felt he had done well by completing the practice examples, with my help.

The test was administered in July 1962, towards the end of the children's third term in school. The results are set out in Table I. Three children were absent when the testing took place and thus only 27 children are shown in the table.

The scores obtained were astonishing. It had been anticipated that a few of the better readers in the class might complete a small number of items correctly. Even this would have been considered an achievement in the circumstances. But the results were

TABLE I

Mean Chronological Age = 5 years 1 month
Mean Raw Score   = 8
Mean Reading Age   = 6 years 3 months

| Child | Chronological Age | | Southgate Test I | |
	Y.	M.	Raw Score	Reading Age Y. M.
1 B	5	2	24	7 5
2 B	5	0	23	7 3
3 G	4	11	18	6 10
4 B	5	2	16	6 9
5 G	5	0	15	6 8
6 G	5	2	13	6 7
7 G	4	11	13	6 7
8 B	5	2	12	6 7
9 B	5	1	11	6 6
10 G	4	11	10	6 5
11 G	5	2	9	6 4
12 G	5	0	9	6 4
13 B	5	1	7	6 2
14 G	5	3	6	6 0
15 B	5	1	5	5 9
16 G	5	2	5	5 9
17 G	5	2	5	5 9
18 G	5	0	4	<5 9
19 G	4	10	4	<5 9
20 B	4	11	4	<5 9
21 G	5	2	2	<5 9
22 B	5	2	1	<5 9
5 children			nil	—

B = boy   G = girl   < = less than

such that, had every child in the class been exactly one year older and had the children been taught to read in traditional print, one would have concluded that they constituted a class of above average intelligence who had made exceptionally good progress in learning to read. When one bears in mind that the average age of these children was between 5 years 0 months and 5 years 1 month (the youngest being 4 years 10 months and the oldest 5 years 3 months), that they had learned to read by means of a different script, that they had not had any training towards transferring to orthodox print and that only two or three children had ever attempted to read traditional print, the results are almost unbelievable.

It will be noted that only five children out of 27 were unable to score on the test. A further five children had raw scores ranging from 4 to 1, which were below the norms for the test. Even these smaller scores had not appeared to me when I observed the children doing the test to be haphazard guesses but rather the results of meaningful choices. The remaining 17 children gained scores which could be converted into Reading Age ranging from 7 years 5 months to 5 years 9 months. It can be noted from the table that of the top ten children, five are boys and five are girls; the same is true of the lowest ten children.

III   THE FOURTH TERM

As the results from the first year's work had been so impressive, the headmistress had agreed to continue the experiment. The class in question moved to a new teacher. Children who had not completed *Janet and John* reading scheme continued with it in the normal way. At the beginning of the autumn term 1962, the class medium of instruction in reading and writing was still A.R. During the term, however, a number of children were considered to be ready to make an official transfer to traditional print. The transfer involved not only providing the children with books printed in orthodox script but it also necessitated the use of a new form of spelling for any writing the teacher put on the blackboard. Thus the teacher frequently found herself doing two different kinds of writing on the board. The children who had 'transferred' were allocated a special blackboard and their words were always written in a different coloured chalk. At this time, as was to be expected, the free writing of children who were making the transfer in reading showed examples of spelling in both alphabets. How long the children will take to make the transfer in spelling is a question which cannot yet be answered. By the end of December 1962, six children were reading nothing but traditional print in school.

TABLE II

Mean Chronological Age = 5 years 6 months
Mean Raw Score   = 14
Mean Reading Age   = 6 years 8 months

Southgate Test I Reading Ages Y. M.	No. of Children
7 9	3
7 7'	2
7 3	1
7 0	2
6 11	1
6 9	5
6 8	2
6 7	1
6 6	1
6 5	2
6 4	2
6 3	2
6 2	2
6 0	1
No score	3

At the end of the autumn term 1962, the children were again tested, using a parallel form of *Southgate Group Reading Test One —Word Selection Test*. On this occasion all 30 of the children in the class were present. The results are summarized in Table II.

It will be seen that a steady improvement had been made during the term. Although only six children had been reading

traditional print in school, 27 children were able to score on the
test. (The children who had made the transfer were the first five
children in Table II, together with one child who scored a Reading
Age of 6 years 9 months.) The mean chronological age of the
class was just less than 5 years 6 months; apart from three children
who could not manage the test, the remaining 27 children in the
class attained Reading Ages of 6 years 0 months and over. The
scores of the highest two children went beyond the table of norms
for the test, representing Reading Ages greater than 7 years 9
months. At the lower end of the list, it was interesting to note
that the five children whose scores in July had been 4, 4, 4, 2 and 1
now registered scores of 17, 9, 8, 7 and 10 respectively, representing Reading Ages of 6 years 9 months to 6 years 2 months.

TABLE III

Child	Chronological Age Y. M.		Reading Ages in Years and Months	
			Southgate Test 1	Southgate Test 2
1 B	5	7	>7 9	8 3
3 G	5	4	>7 9	7 10
6 G	5	7	7 9	7 9
4 B	5	7	7 7	7 9
2 B	5	5	7 7	8 4
12 G	5	5	7 3	7 2
13 B	5	6	7 0	—
9 B	5	6	7 0	7 2
5 G	5	5	6 11	7 3

B = boy   G = girl   > = greater than

As *Southgate Group Reading Test One* had not proved sufficiently difficult to extend two of the children, and as nearly a third
of the class showed Reading Ages of seven and over, it was
decided that the nine children who headed the list might attempt
Southgate Group Reading Test Two—Sentence Completion Test
(Southgate 1962). This test, which was designed to follow Test
One with a slight overlap, was intended to be used mainly with

seven- and eight-year-olds. It was found that only one of the selected nine children was unable to score on the test. The others gained scores equivalent to Reading Ages of 8 years 3 months to 7 years 2 months. Three of these children were still reading books in A.R., not having yet made the transfer to traditional script. The results are set out in Table III (page 80).

IV   CONCLUSIONS

It is certain that no definite conclusions about the value of A.R. as a means of teaching reading can be drawn until the children in the experimental classes are considerably older, perhaps even until they have reached the upper end of the primary school. Furthermore, at that stage, one would wish to consider the published results and the experimental design of the current widespread experiments into the use of this alphabet before one could attempt a final appraisal. Nevertheless, my continued observations of one class in the experiment, considered alongside the results of tests in traditional print, lead me to put forward the following tentative conclusions.

1.   Children in this reception class learned to read at an earlier age than usual.
2.   The process of learning to read took place in a much shorter space of time than is usual.
3.   As a result of points 1 and 2, children aged from four to five and a half years were much more interested in reading and read very many more books than is usual with children of this age.
4.   The successful use of A.R. suggests that most young children are able to make finer visual and auditory discriminations than has commonly been supposed.
5.   Listening to the children reading, talking to them about what they had read and considering the test results in Table III, all suggest that the children's understanding tends to keep pace with their ability to pronounce the words which they are reading.
6.   Free writing in the class appeared more spontaneous, prolific and correctly spelt than is usual with such young children.

7.   All the indications are that the anticipated problem of making the transfer from A.R. to traditional print is one which exists in the mind of the adult rather than one which causes a practical stumbling block to the child.

ADDENDA

1.   The Augmented Roman Alphabet (later renamed the Initial Teaching Alphabet) was devised by Sir James Pitman as a means of simplifying the initial stages of learning to read. See:

   PITMAN, J. (1959) *The Ehrhardt Augmented (40-sound 42-character) Lower-case Roman Alphabet.* London: Pitman.

In 1960 the Institute of Education of the University of London in association with the National Foundation for Educational Research, and with the approval of the Ministry of Education, undertook to set up an experiment to test the effectiveness of this new alphabet with infants. The experiment began in September 1961 under the direction of John Downing. This particular experiment is now usually referred to as 'The first British experiment with i.t.a.'.

2.   In 1959 the Augmented Roman Alphabet contained 42 characters, but by the time the first British experiment commenced in 1961 one additional character had been added to make 43. One further character was introduced later so that i.t.a. now consists of 44 characters.

3.   The article which forms the content of this chapter was written early in 1963. During the course of 1963 and 1964 many lectures were delivered and many books and articles published, giving the results of the first British experiment with i.t.a. Among the publications were Downing (1963a and b), Downing (1964a, b, c and d), Georgiades (1963) and Harrison (1964). These were all written by people closely connected with the experiment. Moreover, they were reports of interim results, being published before exact details of the experimental design had been disclosed—a most unusual procedure in the field of educational research, where it is generally accepted that the results of an experiment can only be meaningfully interpreted when its

details have been fully reported, in such a manner as to enable those competent to do so to assess the appropriateness of its design and conduct. Normally, the publication of such a report, on the completion of an educational experiment, provides the researcher responsible for the experiment with an opportunity to discuss his results in the light of the variables within the situation which he was able to control, as well as his awareness of the relative importance of those variables he was unable to control. Thus the final conclusions drawn by the researcher from his results are based on the breadth of his appreciation, and the soundness of his interpretation, of the totality of factors existing in the situation in which the experiment was conducted.

In the circumstances in which results relating to the i.t.a. experiment were being published, and the unprecedented publicity accompanying them, I became concerned lest teachers might accept these interim results as conclusive evidence of the efficacy of i.t.a. in comparison with current and possible future ways of using traditional orthography (t.o.). It would not have been surprising if teachers, most of whom would not claim to be trained as research workers, had not fully appreciated that the exceptionally good results being published might be at least partially attributable to certain circumstances relating to the experiment, other than the introduction of the new orthography.

Accordingly, in 1964 I wrote an article drawing attention to some of the factors that might have helped to boost the results in experimental classes and, in particular, I developed the concept of a 'reading drive'. This article, 'Approaching i.t.a. Results with Caution', was published in February 1965 and is reprinted as Chapter 6 of this book. In it I was not attempting to prove that children were not doing well with i.t.a., for I had personally observed excellent progress being made in many schools, but rather to suggest that the earliest published results might very well be due to a combination of exceptional circumstances. In the event, later test results and reports confirmed that this was so as, although other classes using i.t.a. in the second and third years of the experiment made good progress, the results rarely reached the level of reading attainments of the children who formed the experimental classes in the first year of the experiment.

6 Approaching i.t.a. Results with Caution

An article published in EDUCATIONAL RESEARCH, *Volume 7, 83–96, February 1965, and later reprinted in* READING RESEARCH QUARTERLY *Volume 1, No. 3, 35–56, Spring 1966.*

I INTRODUCTION

The first British experiment with the Initial Teaching Alphabet (i.t.a.), conducted by Downing, commenced in September 1961 and has now been running for 3 years. As numerous reports noting the successful use of i.t.a. have already been published, for example, Pitman (1961), Downing (1962a), Downing (1962b), Downing and Gardner (1962), Downing (1963a), Georgiades (1963), Southgate (1963), Downing (1964a), Downing (1964b), Downing (1964c) and Harrison (1964), it is probably timely to attempt a sober appraisal of what the results of this research project might really mean.

One of the difficulties in such an attempt is that full details of the experimental design have not yet been released. However, published descriptions of the design and personal observations of the experiment in progress yield the following information. The augmented alphabet, consisting of 43 characters, designed by Sir James Pitman, is intended for use in the early stages of learning to read. The alphabet was first known as the 'Augmented Roman Alphabet' but was later renamed the 'Initial Teaching Alphabet'.

This first experiment to test the effectiveness of the new alphabet follows the pattern of matched experimental and control classes. Both groups are using *Janet and John* (O'Donnell and

84

Munro 1949) as the basic reading scheme: the control classes use the scheme in its standard form, while the experimental classes have editions printed in i.t.a. Teachers in both groups have been requested to continue with their former methods of teaching reading.

The experiment commenced with children aged four and five years who were new entrants to infant schools. The original experimental classes comprised some 400 children in 20 schools in six different local education authorities. Control classes were selected in the same areas, the number of children being almost twice as large as in the experimental classes. (Numbers quoted in published tables of results for these original children vary from 332 to 435 for experimental groups and from 623 to 821 for control groups.) Neither the method of selecting the experimental and control classes in these areas, nor information as to whether the groups may be considered representative samples of the relevant populations, has yet been disclosed. In the two years following the commencement of the experiment, further schools continued to be added to both groups until by 1963 there were over 100 experimental schools using the alphabet with new entrants. i.t.a. was also being used for remedial reading in 65 centres. Two years after the experiment had begun, the matching of control and experimental groups had not been completed, although some matching for age, sex, intelligence and social class had taken place.

The provision of equipment differs for experimental and control classes. Most of the control classes were already using the *Janet and John* reading scheme in the standard edition and so continued to use books already in the school. It is not known whether every class has the full complement of supplementary books and apparatus for this scheme, nor the extent of their additional book corner material. The experimental classes have been supplied with complete new *Janet and John* schemes, including supplementary books and apparatus, all printed in i.t.a. They have also received stocks of new books for the book corners.

Prior to taking part in the experiment, teachers in the experimental classes attended special two-day training workshops in the use of i.t.a. During the course of the experiment, they attended regular monthly meetings to consider problems and discuss progress. They were first supplied with pamphlets about i.t.a., and later with a bulletin entitled *i.t.a. journal*. Every parent of a child using i.t.a. was given a booklet about the new alphabet, the experiment was discussed at parent teacher meetings and parents were encouraged to buy i.t.a. books or borrow them from public libraries. Some attempt was made to arrange lectures and meetings for teachers of control classes but the total stimulus in this context was not large.

Many children in experimental classes made rapid progress and results began to be published in November 1962 (Downing and Gardner 1962) and have continued ever since. A great deal of publicity has been given in the press, on television and by means of a film and lectures, to the progress made by children using i.t.a.

The duration of the experiment has not been indicated although Downing (1964a), reporting on the achievements of the first two years of the experiment, says: 'It will be necessary to follow these children for several years to determine their ultimate reading status.'

Few people would now doubt that many children using i.t.a. in these experiments have learned to read earlier, more easily and more speedily than their teachers expected and that this performance is better than the average normal class's attainment in reading. Numerous publications on this theme have appeared and, while the statistical comparisons leave something to be desired, the general impression of increased performance can be accepted. The writer's own observations and independent testing (Southgate 1963) confirm this trend.

Nevertheless there are dangers of teachers being so impressed by these reports of success that they fail to appreciate that statements of dramatic results refer to particular and very special conditions and are not necessarily applicable to the teaching of reading in general. The results from the present experimental classes cannot be taken to indicate that the wholesale adoption of i.t.a. would necessarily lead to a raising of reading standards greater than would the adoption of some other reading approach, if it were tried out under conditions similar to those which have been prevalent in i.t.a. classes.

II THE EFFECT OF A 'READING DRIVE'

It should be pointed out that however good the results in the experimental classes, there is the possibility that they could be accounted for, either wholly or partially, by factors other than the introduction of a new alphabet. The main factor is the effects of what might be termed a 'drive' in the teaching of reading. A 'reading drive' is a fairly common phenomenon which takes place at irregular intervals in many schools, classes and remedial groups, regardless of whether the group is taking part in an experiment or being closely watched by others. Certainly, the drive may be intensified if public interest is added to it. A reading drive is an extremely potent force which, at any one time, can produce praiseworthy results, often in obscurity, in a large number of schools in the country.

A reading drive is basically a new surge of inspiration through the teaching of the subject. It ferments in the teacher and bubbles over on to the children who are thrust forward on its waves of enthusiasm. The drive is accompanied by an increase in interest, motivation and application which is inevitably followed by an improvement in attainments. A reading drive can stem from one ingredient or from a combination of many ingredients. These may include a new teacher or headteacher, a new scheme or method, new books, new apparatus, a new library, testing, recording, regrouping or cross-classification of children, lectures and discussion groups for teachers.

Before examining more closely some of the factors which can contribute towards a reading drive, one important point relating to teachers in primary schools should be kept in mind. The teacher in the primary school, and more particularly in an infant class, being concerned with so many aspects of the child's day, can never be expected to be functioning at optimum level on all fronts at any one time. There are always aspects of the curriculum which, because of individual preference or current interest on the part of the teacher, are given most attention and other aspects which are relegated to a lower order of priority. An example of the former is the teacher whose personal preference is

for art and craft, and who may give only moderate attention to
reading and mathematics. The approach of Christmas, when a
surge of activities centring on this theme usually results in a
temporary decline in more formal work, offers an example of
the latter.

The headteacher in the primary school usually bears even
more responsibility than the class teacher for the emphasis which
is placed on different aspects of the curriculum. Any inspector or
adviser could cite examples of pairs of schools in similar areas,
one of which has achieved high standards in a particular subject and
the other in which the same subject is merely average or below. The
difference often lies in the beliefs of the respective headteachers.
The one who believes that the teaching of reading must have
first priority has a permanent reading drive in force in his school.
The writer, having been concerned for a number of years in a
remedial and advisory service, has experienced numerous examples
of increased reading ability resulting from reading drives which
were instigated by newly appointed teachers or headteachers.
These drives have achieved good results, almost irrespective of the
reading schemes or methods with which they were associated;
indeed, often no change in books or method of teaching was
made.

Courses of lectures to teachers, especially lectures dealing
with practical problems of teaching reading to classes in which
wide ranges of reading ability exist, have resulted in overall
gains in reading attainment. In some schools, grouping of children
within a class according to reading attainments has produced good
results, as has cross-classification for reading throughout a school.
In other cases, the pooling and careful grading of all reading books
in the school, enabling teachers to supply children with ample
books at each reading level, brought a new surge forward in
reading ability. Placing retarded children in remedial reading
groups has also been found to be accompanied by an improvement in the reading ability of other children in the same school
(Birch 1953).

One simple example of a reading drive concerns an infant
school in which the reading standards were very low and the
teachers, realizing this, asked to have discussions on the subject.

The school had been using the *Janet and John* reading scheme. In the first discussion the teachers' initial reaction was to enquire about the possibility of a 'better' reading scheme. They were persuaded to retain the same scheme but to make better use of it. It was found that only one teacher knew that a teacher's manual for the scheme existed and no teacher had read it. It was also discovered that reading periods were often missed because of lengthy assemblies or the collection of dinner money and savings. Many other deficiencies came to light in discussion and a more systematic plan for reading tuition in the school was evolved. As might be expected, within a year or two there was a vast improvement in the reading standards in the school.

A second example concerns a mixed junior school. The mean Reading Age of its first-year intake of 140 children was only 6 years 5 months (mean Chronological Age 7 years 6 months). The urgency of the situation demanded an immediate and powerful reading drive, but precluded the possibility of ordering new books or considering new methods. The intake was divided into four classes according to reading ability or lack of it. The books already in the school had to be used; they comprised a variety of reading schemes and supplementary books which were far from perfect for the task. The children who had begun to read were placed in the first two classes and grouped for reading practice according to reading ability. The two lower classes had to make a completely new beginning in reading and at first this involved class teaching. Although no new, spectacular ideas were tried out, the reading drive did at least ensure that some reading teaching and reading practice took place every day. As a result, the mean Reading Age for the whole age group rose by 1 year 6 months in 9 months. In the same period, a reading drive with the second year juniors produced a mean gain of two years (from mean Reading Age of 7 years 5 months to mean Reading Age of 9 years 5 months). It is worth emphasizing that these results refer to complete age-groups of children, which included some educationally sub-normal children as well as certain bright children who were not retarded in reading. Thus, average gains of two years conceal some individual gains of three and four years.

One further example illustrates that a reading drive can be

effective even when made by inexperienced teachers. A new
secondary modern school had a first year intake of 177 boys and
girls. The mean Chronological Age of the group was 11 years 5
months and the mean Reading Age 10 years 4 months. The
entire intake was cross-classified for English and mathematics.
The English groups were based on reading ages and, for all
except the top group, a drive towards teaching reading went
into effect. No teacher in the school had previous experience of
teaching reading; those teaching reading were specialist teachers of
such subjects as needlework, music, geography and religious
instruction. It is all the more remarkable that in 10 months the
mean Reading Age of the whole intake, apart from the top
group who were not retarded and thus were not included in the
reading drive, went up by two years.

Of all the means available to an adviser or headteacher who
wishes to initiate a reading drive in a school, the introduction of
brand new books must be rated most highly. Nothing is more
likely to give the teacher a new surge of interest in the subject.
We know what a new reading scheme can do for the failing
reader; it can act similarly on the flagging teacher. Practically all
primary classes contain pupils who have failed to read or who read
less well than their teacher desires. It is of these children the teacher
is usually thinking when she tries a different reading scheme or
method, and the fillip of having a new reading scheme or new
books in the book corner is tremendous for the teacher, as well as
for the children.

It may be that too much attention has been given to method
or medium in the question of learning to read and too little
attention to the teacher. Experience of improvements in reading
standards in many schools, using a large variety of approaches,
suggests that drive and determination on the part of the teacher
is a more important factor than the selection of any particular
approach to reading. Certainly some teachers possess more skill
in teaching reading than do others, but a reading drive can
engender such enthusiasm, even in teachers whose skill in teaching
reading is meagre or non-existent, that reading progress will be
greatly accelerated.

III READING DRIVE AND THE HAWTHORNE EFFECT

A reading drive is not the same concept as the 'Hawthorne effect' although there are certain common features. The 'Hawthorne effect' derives its name from experiments carried out in Massachusetts, in 1924, with workers in the Hawthorne plant of the Western Electric Company. The original experiment was designed to ascertain the relationship between illumination and production in a variety of factory conditions but the experiments were later extended to include other variables. The series of experiments showed that better lighting, rest periods and wage incentives, as well as poorer lighting, longer hours, no rest periods or lunch hours, all led to greater productivity in experimental and control groups alike. The investigators were forced to conclude that increased productivity resulted from the operation of social factors, and it was left to later commentators to assert that the operative factor was, without doubt, the knowledge on the part of the workers that they were involved in an experiment and were being observed. Cook (1962) defines the 'Hawthorne effect' as follows. 'The "Hawthorne effect" is a phenomenon characterized by an awareness on the part of the subjects of special treatment created by artificial experimental conditions. This awareness becomes confounded with the independent variable under study, with a subsequent facilitating effect on the dependent variable, thus leading to ambiguous results.'

Three features of these experiments require stressing. The variables under examination were only indirectly related to the dependent variable—productivity. The girls in the factory were not being urged to increase production nor were they being trained to do their jobs in a new way with the aim of improving performance; in fact, no production drive was in force. The extraneous variables were being examined because of a hypothesis that they might have direct bearing on the dependent variable. In the event, an unsuspected indirect variable was discovered which seriously influenced the dependent variable in a favourable direction. Secondly, productivity increased in both control and experimental groups. Thirdly, the awareness of being observed appeared to result in increased output almost without conscious effort.

Educational experiments in which the results of new ways of instruction used in experimental groups are compared with accepted ways of teaching used in control groups differ from the Hawthorne experiments in certain respects. In the educational experiment, the variable factor is not extraneous to the situation but an intrinsic part of the process which is under consideration. In this case the variable is the method or medium of teaching that skill which will later be tested. Such an experiment must of necessity create in the experimental groups a drive in the factor concerned; for instance a reading drive. In the Hawthorne experiment no specific productivity drive was in force in the experimental groups.

In these educational experiments, as both control and experimental groups become aware that performance in a particular subject is being observed, there are likely to be increases in performance. In so far as these gains are achieved without conscious volition on the part of the teachers and pupils, they are the true 'Hawthorne effects' in such experiments.

However, in experiments concerning the teaching of reading, the members of experimental groups must have more than just an awareness of being observed. There is conscious motivation for increased performance, stemming from the reading drive. The teacher trying a new approach to reading in an experimental class is certainly conscious of a drive towards better performance. Any unconscious motivation in the children attributable to the 'Hawthorne effect' would be increased in the experimental classes as a result of the reading drive. The more than usual pleasure and approval of the teacher when good progress is made may well raise the children's motivation to a conscious level.

Thus, in educational experiments concerned with teaching techniques, Hawthorne effects are likely to be present in both experimental and control classes. If greater publicity and attention is given to the experimental classes the Hawthorne effects may be increased, but we have no means of gauging this. An additional and much more potent factor in respect of progress in reading is the reading drive which must inevitably be in force in the experimental classes.

IV   OTHER APPROACHES TO THE TEACHING OF READING

The author or originator of any new approach to reading usually claims that excellent results have been obtained in the classroom situation before the scheme was marketed. One need not be cynical about such claims from authors as their own drive and enthusiasm has usually been so marked in the experimental stages that children's progress has been far above average.

In the past fifteen years or so many such schemes have been put forward, some intended for use with infants and some for older children who were failing in reading. Among these may be mentioned *Active Reading* (Miles 1951), *Adventures in Reading and Writing* (Keir 1947), *Fun with Phonics* (Reis 1962), *A Remedial Reading Method* (Moxon 1962), *Programmed Reading Kit* (Stott 1962), *Royal Road Readers* (Daniels and Diack 1957), *Sound Sense* (Tansley 1961), *Sounds and Words* (Southgate and Havenhand 1959), and *Words in Colour* (Gattegno 1962). The most recent approaches are i.t.a., various linguistic approaches to the teaching of reading, and the use of teaching machines.

The results obtained by ordinary teachers, with ordinary classes, using one of these approaches, will be likely to be less spectacular than those claimed by the initiators of the idea. Three reasons for this can be suggested. First, it is unlikely that the teacher will be able to put into the effort the same spurt of driving force as the initiator. Secondly, it is probable that the teacher may not have available all the supporting equipment or books. Thirdly, it is rare to find a new approach being used exactly as the author planned, and deviations from the author's plan are more often a detriment than an asset to the scheme. On the other hand, when a teacher first uses an entirely new approach to reading, the results are likely to be a considerable improvement on previous ones. Many teachers using new schemes can produce test results to substantiate their own feelings that the new approach is 'better'. Unfortunately these test results do

not show whether the teacher was teaching better because a
reading drive had been sparked off by the stimulus of a new
scheme, whether the children were learning more because their
teacher was inspired and they were more highly motivated, or
whether the scheme *per se* could be credited with the acceleration
in learning. Nor do we usually know what the new approach
was being measured against.

Schemes used for remedial teaching are particularly suscept-
ible to these snags. Practically any of the foregoing approaches,
used by a reasonably keen remedial teacher, will produce even
more spectacular results than with normal classes of infants or
juniors. So will a reading drive with retarded or backward
readers which uses old-fashioned books, no books, children's
home-made books, the Fernald-Keller method (Fernald 1943),
or what you will. The results merely show that when teachers
are inspired to help children to learn to read, reading progress
will be accelerated.

Such results, obtained by so many schools and remedial services, and relating to so many different reading approaches, are
rarely published except in author's manuals for reading schemes
or in publishers' advertising leaflets. In these circumstances, the results are merely used to illustrate the advantages of the approach
in question and not to form a comparison with the results gained
by the use of alternative approaches. It is unfortunate that there is
a dearth of published accounts of work in both normal classes and
remedial groups comparing different approaches, with a view to
indicating the superiority of any one approach over the
others.

Daniels and Diack (1956 and 1960) report that what they
term 'the phonic word method', as exemplified in the *Royal
Road Readers*, showed considerable improvement over what they
term 'mixed methods'. Referring to children who have spent two
years in the infant school they also say (1956), 'The superiority
in reading progress of the school using the Phonic-Word Method
over the other four schools taken together cannot be estimated at
less than nine months of reading age . . .'. Although it could be
suggested that a two-year teaching programme with the new
approach of the *Royal Road Readers* constituted a reading drive,

in contrast to the 'mixed method' schools, it is difficult to imagine that it produced the sort of drive now taking place in i.t.a. classes. In these circumstances, the gains compare favourably with the gains in i.t.a. classes. Yet there still remains the possibility that the use of other approaches would result in similar gains over 'mixed methods'. The answer is just not known because appropriate pieces of research, attempting to compare one particular approach with other approaches, have not been carried out. The reason for this gap can probably be traced to the lack of financial assistance for what would be a difficult, long-term and expensive piece of research.

One further claim made by some authors, as well as by teachers who have used new approaches to reading, refers to the marked improvements in the children's behaviour and in their attitude to reading, to school work, to adults and children, and to life in general. One would not dispute this, but it is not a phenomenon which is unique to i.t.a., nor to any other specific approach. It is equally applicable to children who have learned to read in any way whatsoever and it is particularly true of backward and retarded readers who have received remedial teaching and made good reading progress.

V   THE MAGNITUDE OF THE READING DRIVE IN i.t.a.

In assessing the results of a new reading approach, it is obviously extremely important to realize that any 'drive' in the subject is likely to bring about increased performance. In appraising the results obtained by classes using i.t.a., we cannot afford to discount the fact that there has never been in this country a drive in the teaching of reading in any way approaching the magnitude of the current drive. It is worth looking closely at the many strands which contribute to it.

The i.t.a. classes have teachers who are stimulated by the idea of experimenting with a new approach. These teachers are further stimulated by lectures or talks given by the originators of the new alphabet. Teachers in normal classes lack the drive given by the possibility of trying out a new approach and only rarely have the opportunity of being stimulated by the authors of a new scheme.

Teachers in the experimental classes go to i.t.a. workshops and study how to use the new alphabet; they read books and pamphlets about i.t.a. and have regular discussions with each other about problems arising in connection with their work. They even have a journal devoted entirely to i.t.a. In effect, one of the roles played by workshops, lectures, discussions and pamphlets is the training of teachers to improve that very skill which will later be measured. It seems fair to assume that teachers who have undergone such training and received such support and encouragement are better teachers of reading than they were before they took part in the experiment. They have certainly thought about what they are trying to do and they know something about the teaching of reading. All teachers in normal infant classes are not necessarily in this position. The situation described earlier, in which teachers in an infant school had not read the manual for the *Janet and John* reading scheme and thus were not using the scheme to the best advantage, is not unusual. Furthermore, of the teachers now in infant schools, far more than is commonly supposed appear to have received little training in the teaching of reading. This aspect of the training of teachers in experimental classes increases the strong reading drive which is motivating them and so places them in a favourable position compared with teachers in control classes.

In addition to the excitement of trying out a new way of teaching reading, the teachers in the experimental classes were provided with new books and apparatus for a complete reading scheme—a rare event in any infant class. At the same time they acquired stocks of new books for the library corner. The prospect of having a new reading scheme, new books in the library corner and a new alphabet, all at the same time, must have proved incalculably exhilarating to the teacher and likely to have completely revitalized her teaching. One cannot assess how far such a drive alone could have succeeded in raising reading standards. The control class, on the other hand, did not start off with a new approach nor with a new reading scheme and books for the library corner.

The i.t.a. classes have had visitors showing an interest in their reading progress. In some of these schools there has been a moderate number of visitors, but in others the stream of visitors has almost amounted to a flood. Normal classes only rarely have visitors showing an interest in reading progress. Some of the control classes have had occasional visitors; many have had no visitors.

Seeing test results which indicate that good progress is being made is in itself a powerful incentive. The i.t.a. classes have had this in abundance. What effect the early publication of comparative results between experimental and control classes may have had on the teaching of reading in the control classes, we do not know. It seems obvious that the teachers in the i.t.a. classes cannot fail to have been encouraged by the many publications which have reiterated the success of i.t.a. Never has there been a new idea in reading which has produced so many reports, not only in the educational press but also in the popular press. There have been the further powerful factors of a film and many television interviews.

As has been suggested earlier, any one of the factors which contributes to a reading drive can produce reading gains: a number of these factors used in conjunction can produce powerful results. The experimental classes in the i.t.a. research have utilised, perhaps without even realizing it, most of the contributory factors mentioned.

The results from the i.t.a. classes demonstrate that, given a massive drive in teaching reading, including new books and all other methods of arousing enthusiasm in teachers, learning to read can be accelerated and the standards raised, but they do not help us to decide whether these results are attributable to the drive itself or to the teaching approach used. This is a question which the thinking teacher cannot ignore.

VI   THE HAWTHORNE EFFECT IN THE i.t.a. EXPERIMENT

When the i.t.a. experiment commenced, though much thought was given to the possibilities of the Hawthorne effect, there seems to have been little awareness of how powerful a reading drive might prove to be. Downing (1964a) says: 'These control schools have been provided with refresher courses and their teachers attend regular meetings to discuss research in order to match the Hawthorne effect which may be generated by the training and research meetings of the i.t.a. teachers. In this and in other ways care has been taken to provide comparable situations in i.t.a. and control classes.' Observers cannot help but suggest that although it has been claimed (Downing 1964c) that 'every effort has been made to achieve a balance' (that is, with regard to the Hawthorne effect), it has not been entirely successful. Few refresher courses have been provided for teachers in control schools nor have 'regular meetings' been usual. One can appreciate that teachers of control classes who were not willing volunteers, and many were not, were unlikely to respond fully to invitations to attend lectures and meetings. Even when such functions *were* attended by control classes teachers, the stimulus would fall far short of that generated by discussions relating to an entirely new approach to reading. In practice, teachers of control classes seem to have proceeded very much as usual, few of them becoming involved in lectures, refresher courses or regular meetings. Similarly, in the case of another aspect of the Hawthorne effect, if equality of visitors and publicity was actually aimed at for experimental and control schools, it is doubtful whether this was achieved.

Although both Hawthorne effect and reading drive must be at work in the i.t.a. experiment, it is not easy to draw an absolutely clear demarcation line because many of the factors in the situation play double or even treble roles. It has already been suggested that testing, lectures, meetings, publications, visitors and publicity are likely to have produced Hawthorne effects in both control and experimental groups and that, in so far as the experimental groups have received greater stimulus, there exists the possibility that the Hawthorne effect may be greater in the experimental classes. Also, many of the same factors are directly relevant to a reading drive; lectures, discussions, workshops, pamphlets, reports and publicity come into this category. In addition some of these factors also constitute specific training for the teachers which will strengthen the reading drive. As the attempt to stimulate control schools was not very successful, it is hardly likely that a reading drive was in force in the control schools or that the training of teachers in the techniques of teaching reading has been affected.

Two further points relating to the training of teachers in these experiments need clarifying. When teachers are given direct training in teaching reading, as were those in charge of experimental classes, the results cannot really be attributed to the Hawthorne effect, but are much more clearly in line with the concept of reading drive. It is also difficult to imagine that teachers who have undergone such training would not in some measure change 'their usual methods of teaching'. It is unrealistic to take for granted that because teachers of both control and experimental classes were asked not to change their methods they are still proceeding exactly as formerly. Furthermore, if the training of teachers in control groups had become a feasible proposition, their methods of teaching would also have been likely to undergo some change.

What has not been made clear is whether the 'control classes' were intended as control groups proper or whether they were envisaged as second experimental groups. This is a crucial point which needs to be clarified before the two sets of figures can reasonably be compared. If they are control groups proper, it may be suggested that nothing aimed at boosting performance should have been attempted. On the other hand, if these 'control classes' are going to be considered as *experimental* classes (whose reading drive was to have been equated with the drive already described in the i.t.a. classes), the treatment should have been identical in every respect save one, the use of i.t.a. The treatment which has been given to the control classes falls short, in new books and equipment, in lectures and discussions, in visitors and publicity.

VII A SUGGESTION FOR CONTROLLING READING DRIVE
     IN i.t.a. EXPERIMENTS

Any experiment devised to test the efficacy of a new approach to reading cannot afford to neglect the concept of a reading drive.

Such an experiment would need to have more than one set of experimental groups and should, ideally, investigate at least two new approaches to reading concurrently. All-embracing arrangements to ensure equivalent drive in all experimental groups would need to be made and rigidly adhered to. In addition, there should be control groups which are not tampered with. This suggests an experiment somewhat along the following lines. (For the sake of simplicity, it is here assumed that *Janet and John* is the basic reading scheme.)

Experimental Group 1 would consist of classes using *Janet and John* reading scheme and additional books printed in i.t.a. Experimental Group 2 would use *Janet and John* reading scheme and other books in traditional orthography. Experimental Group 3 (and other additional experimental groups decided upon) would use some other *systematic* method of teaching reading: for example, *Fun with Phonics* (Reis 1962), *Programmed Reading Kit* (Stott 1962), *Royal Road Readers* (Daniels and Diack 1957), or *Words in Colour* (Gattegno 1962). The control group would comprise classes in which there was to be no change from their normal methods or books. It would be preferable for these classes not to know that they were part of the control group. If testing for all groups were cut to a minimum, it should be possible to select control groups from local education authorities where the testing of intelligence and reading ability is carried out at regular intervals as a matter of routine. The classes selected would then form a true control group. The possibility of the results being affected by either the Hawthorne effect or a reading drive attributable to the experiment would be excluded.

The selection of classes for the experimental groups might be arranged in the following manner. In each selected area, a course of lectures on 'The choice of an approach to the teaching of reading' could be arranged. The course would be open to those headteachers, accompanied by one or more members of their staffs, who were eager to experiment with a new reading approach. The course would, at successive meetings, offer the authors or supporters of each selected approach the opportunity of 'selling' their idea to the audience. One meeting at least would be also devoted to someone talking about using *Janet and John* to the best advantage.

At the conclusion of the course, lists would be made of those schools in which the headteacher and staff wanted to experiment with a particular approach. Only schools which had not previously used the *Janet and John* traditional scheme would be eligible for inclusion in Experimental Group 2. There would certainly be no lack of volunteers for each approach. The actual experimental groups could then be selected from among these volunteers, according to the other criteria necessitated by the experimental design. This plan would have the advantage of ensuring that each experimental class was staffed by a keen teacher strongly supported by the headteacher.

Equivalent drive in each group would then be ensured by absolute parity of treatment throughout the duration of the experiment. Each experimental group, including the one using traditional *Janet and John*, would be provided with complete sets of the new books and apparatus which form part of the scheme. Equal numbers of supporting books would be provided for the book corners.

All the teachers in an area who comprised one experimental group would have meetings before and during the experiment to discuss their problems and progress. The incentive of experimenting with a new approach to reading would be likely to encourage teachers to attend such meetings. The 'we-feeling', resulting from the new experience the teachers were sharing, would be likely to develop into the sort of friendly club feeling which has been engendered by i.t.a. meetings. Morale would consequently be high.

Visitors who would applaud reading progress would visit all the experimental classes although not, one would hope, in such large numbers as have visited some of the i.t.a. classes. Publicity given to one approach would be given equally to the others, although one would hope that it would be reduced to a minimum.

With reading drives organized in this way, improvement in reading attainments in all the experimental classes would be likely to be large as compared with the control group. These gains would illustrate the progress in learning to read that children can make when their teachers are filled with enthusiasm and are encouraged and supported by the provision of adequate books and equipment. Comparisons between the results of the different experimental groups would be of paramount interest, whether they proved large or, as they might well do, insignificant, and would demonstrate differences directly attributable to the approaches employed.

It might be said that the type of experiment suggested here would have required more money for new books and equipment than was available at the commencement of the first British i.t.a. experiment. Such a response would contain a good deal of truth. Even so, it is worth remembering that a small, well-designed experiment may produce more valuable results than a much larger experiment more loosely designed. An increase in the number of subjects in an experiment cannot increase the validity of results if the original design of the experiment is not fully adequate.

VIII POINTS TO BE CONSIDERED BY THE TEACHER

The prudent headteacher who is considering the possibility of using i.t.a. will no doubt give careful thought to the matter before he takes the decision. He may feel that he would prefer to wait until the original children are ten or eleven years old before attempting to appraise the results. At that stage more definite results for the slower children using i.t.a. may have become available, this being the acid test of a new approach to reading, as far as many teachers are concerned.

The following questions are also among those on which a headteacher might ponder. What could be achieved by a reading drive, using the books that are at present in the school? How much would complete sets of i.t.a. books and equipment, including books for the book corner, cost? If it is intended to spend this sum of money on a new reading approach, are there other approaches producing good results which have not received the publicity of i.t.a.? What are the advantages and disadvantages of these approaches compared with the i.t.a. approach? On the other hand, what might be the results of spending even half this amount of money on new books and apparatus to expand and supplement the present scheme? Is it possible that the purchase of supplementary phonic material and the allocation of a short daily period to phonic training might produce an equal increase in the rate of learning to read?

A second set of questions refers particularly to infant schools. Is the school in an area where there is a changing population? In other words, are there large numbers of children either entering or leaving in the middle of the infant school course? If so, will the problems of children who are half way through the process of learning to read, in a different medium, be easy to solve for either the leavers or the new entrants, or will there arise a floating child population who cannot read either i.t.a. or traditional orthography? Similarly, if the junior school fed by the i.t.a. infant school does not have teachers who can use i.t.a., what is going to happen to the children who have not made the transfer to traditional spelling before they are transferred to the junior school?

One further query refers to staffing. The pattern in primary schools in the future, as far as one can foresee, is likely to be one of constantly changing staffs. The percentage of newly-qualified teachers leaving the schools after only a few years of teaching, on account of marriage and child-bearing, is increasing. Some of these teachers may return to teaching after absences of five to twenty years. Many married women returners in infant schools will probably be teachers originally trained for secondary schools and not trained to teach reading. As well as these changes in the permanent staff of infant schools, there is likely to be a great increase in the number of temporary and part-time teachers. In this situation, the headteacher must obviously consider carefully whether newcomers to the staff are more likely to provide continuity of teaching for the children with i.t.a. or with some other approach which uses the traditional alphabet.

IX CONCLUSIONS

i.t.a. is an important and interesting approach to the teaching of reading and many of the schools experimenting with it are achieving exciting results. Yet it is pertinent to remember that as Rosenbloom (1961) points out '... in educational experimentation, no matter what the hypothesis is, the experimental classes do better than the control classes.'

Experience also indicates that any pronounced drive in the teaching of reading produces improvement, almost regardless of the method or scheme employed. It is important to relate this knowledge to the fact that there has never been, in this country, a reading drive which in any way reaches the magnitude of the current one regarding i.t.a. Furthermore, one should bear in mind that there are other approaches to reading which are giving good results but which have not had the opportunities for research and publicity open to i.t.a. Consequently, good results in i.t.a. classes cannot be attributed solely to the new alphabet. Too many other factors are inherent in the situation.

Although many results of the experiment have been published, serious evaluation of them by knowledgeable people is hampered by the fact that a complete statement of the experimental design has not yet been released. Such details of the design as have been published suggest that it will prove impossible to separate gains due to a powerful reading drive, backed by unprecedented publicity, from gains attributable to the alphabet itself. An experiment which compares the results of different reading approaches, in identical circumstances, is urgently needed before an adequate assessment of i.t.a. can be attempted. Until objective data of this sort is available, the possibility cannot be discounted that the results from this first i.t.a. experiment might merely indicate that, when a powerful reading drive is in force, reading progress is accelerated.

ADDENDA

1.   Some of the points raised in the foregoing article were taken up by Downing and Jones in the first article listed below, and a brief reply by the writer was made in the second article:

DOWNING, J. and JONES, B. (1966) 'Some problems of evaluating i.t.a.: A Second Experiment'. *Educational Research*, Vol. 8, No. 2, 100–114.

SOUTHGATE, V. (1967e) 'A few comments on reading drive.' *Educational Research*, Vol. 9. No. 2, 145–6.

It is also interesting to note that more recently, in the following paper, Downing has referred to the article 'Approaching i.t.a. Results with Caution' as being constructive, unbiased and fair-minded:

DOWNING, J. (1971) 'i.t.a.—a review of ten years' research.' In MERRITT, J. E. (ed.) *Reading and the Curriculum*. London: Ward Lock.

2.   The first substantive account of the original British experiment with i.t.a. was given by Downing in the following book:

DOWNING, J. (1967a) *The i.t.a. Symposium* (Research Report on the British Experiment with i.t.a.). Slough: National Foundation for Educational Research.

This volume also contained 'Evaluations on the Report' by twelve well-known educationists.

3.   In the same year, full details of the experimental design, the conduct of the research project and the results obtained were published in:

DOWNING, J. (1967b) *Evaluating the Initial Teaching Alphabet*. London: Cassell.

4.   Meanwhile, in 1965, the Schools Council had invited Professor F. W. Warburton and the writer to undertake an independent evaluation of i.t.a., including an appraisal of published research reports on the use of i.t.a. in both Great Britain and the U.S.A. Downing's first experiment was one of seventeen pieces of research assessed in this evaluation, which was undertaken during 1966 and 1967. The full report was submitted to the Schools Council in 1968 and published in 1969, as follows:

WARBURTON, F. W. and SOUTHGATE, V. (1969) *i.t.a.: An Independent Evaluation*. Edinburgh: Chambers; and London: Murray.

A mini-version of the same report was published in 1970:

SOUTHGATE, V. (1970) *i.t.a. What Is The Evidence?* Edinburgh: Chambers; and London: Murray.

Some of the main findings of this evaluation form the content of Chapter 7 of the current book.

7 An Independent Evaluation of i.t.a.: Sponsored by the Schools Council

A paper presented at the Fifteenth Annual Convention of the International Reading Association, Anaheim, California, May 1970.

I BACKGROUND INFORMATION

The Schools Council, although a British government-sponsored body, is completely independent. Its main purpose is to investigate new developments in schools curricula and examinations in England and Wales, and to co-ordinate and disseminate information. It also arranges programmes of evaluation concerning certain important new projects, in order to provide teachers and other educationists with independent evidence, enabling them to formulate their own answers to the question: 'Can the claims made for this new approach be justified?'

The first evaluation to be initiated by the Schools Council was the independent evaluation of the Initial Teaching Alphabet (i.t.a.) undertaken by Professor Warburton and the writer during 1966–7. The main report of some 200,000 words was published in 1969 (Warburton and Southgate), followed by a mini-version in 1970 (Southgate).

The authors' brief was to collect and evaluate, by means of both measurement and judgement techniques, the available evidence relating to the use of i.t.a. as a means of beginning reading with infants (i.e. five- to seven-year-olds). Their specific terms of reference were threefold: to evaluate published research material on i.t.a. from both Great Britain and the U.S.A., including making an appraisal of the methodology underlying the researches; to collect and evaluate the views of teachers and other knowledgeable people who had been closely connected with i.t.a. in practice; and to suggest future research projects connected with i.t.a., which might be deemed necessary.

Professor Warburton was responsible for the evaluation of research evidence, while the writer investigated the extent of the use of i.t.a. and appraised informed opinion and experience. The authors were faced with many problems: not only was there a vast amount of available evidence but there were serious limitations on time, money and personnel. They emphasize in their report that, although not entirely satisfied with the methods they evolved, they did set out with open minds, to collect as much as possible of the relevant evidence and to evaluate and present it fairly.

As it is clearly impossible even to list all the different facets of this large piece of research in one short paper, the writer mentions only a few selected aspects, mainly from her own sections of the report.

II   THE RESEARCH EVIDENCE

Warburton began his appraisal by devising an ideal experimental design appropriate for researches into classroom teaching of reading. Many of the research reports on i.t.a. which he first examined he discarded as being totally inadequate. The remaining 17 research reports, 11 from the U.S.A., four from England and two from Scotland, he examined in detail.

Each was summarized by asking some 40 questions, based on the ideal experimental design, concerning its scope, design, conduct, techniques and presentation of results. Certain of even these selected pieces of research were found to be badly designed and inadequately reported. For example, even such important information as the timing of the testing, the medium in which the children were tested, and the proportion of children who at the time of testing had made the transition to traditional orthography (t.o.) was sometimes not given or was muddled up.

In these circumstances, Warburton's plan of appraisal enabled him to decide on the relative weighting to be given to the conclusions set out in each piece of research. He ranked most highly Downing's second experiment (Downing and Jones 1966) and the experiments reported by Milne (1966) and Robinson (1966), although unfortunately only interim results were available for these, at that time. In certain researches, with otherwise commendable designs, Warburton considered that the use of different materials and methods confounded the results which might have been attributable to media.

As the principal conclusions drawn from the research evidence were similar to those drawn from the verbal evidence collected by the writer, they are not listed here but the few instances in which the research evidence and verbal evidence differed are noted later.

III   THE EXTENT OF THE USE OF i.t.a.

A questionnaire sent to the 163 local education authorities (L.E.A.s) in England and Wales showed that in 1966, 1,554 schools in 140 L.E.A.s were using i.t.a. to some extent with infants. This represented 9·2% of all schools containing infants. The spread was not even; in one authority all infant schools were using i.t.a., while in others only a few schools were concerned. Only 2% of the schools which had begun to use i.t.a. had discontinued its use. Their reasons for doing so were usually administrative rather than dissatisfaction with the alphabet itself.

In 459 schools i.t.a. was also being used to some extent with junior pupils (aged eight to eleven years) and senior pupils (aged eleven to fifteen years). This figure does not include those junior pupils who were still using i.t.a. as a continuation of their infant reading programme. In addition, in 78 of the local authorities i.t.a. was being used in circumstances other than those already mentioned—for example, in special schools, remedial services and classes for adult illiterates.

IV   THE VERBAL EVIDENCE

While most of the verbal evidence refers to children in English schools, a certain amount arose in interviews and correspondence with teachers and educationists from other countries, including the U.S.A., and from their publications. The writer interviewed nearly 400 people, including teachers, advisers, inspectors, lecturers, educational psychologists, linguists, research workers, parents and publishers. In addition, she visited 46 schools, observed hundreds of children, and talked to them and their teachers.

Time did not permit the employment of a sampling technique for the selection of people to be interviewed. The plan adopted was rather a collection of evidence in pre-determined categories, care being taken to gather divergent opinions within categories when these existed. The steps taken to avoid bias in this procedure are outlined in the report. The advice of local officials and headteachers was sought in order to obtain cross-sections of schools, and of pupils within schools. The interviews were designed to encourage people to express their views freely, regardless of the direction these views might take. The independent nature of the enquiry was emphasized and the fact that all shades of opinion were equally valuable.

1. Mainly favourable impressions of i.t.a.

The majority of the verbal evidence was in favour of i.t.a. as a medium for beginning reading with infants. Only a small minority of those interviewed expressed unfavourable opinions or doubts. The most noticeable trend in this mass of evidence was that the people most experienced about actual teaching and learning in infant classes were most enthusiastic, while those who had misgivings were generally people who had neither taught children to read by means of i.t.a. nor closely observed it in use.

The majority group favouring i.t.a. consisted of most of the teachers who had used it, a large percentage of H. M. Inspectors, many but not all of those local advisers experienced in observing i.t.a. and most of the parents concerned.

The minority group, who were not so impressed by i.t.a. and some of whom were 'anti-i.t.a.', included teachers in schools already achieving satisfactory reading standards with t.o., certain of H.M. Inspectors and local authority inspectors, College and

University lecturers with little first-hand experience of i.t.a. and a few parents. In this group were also found linguists, people who preferred other media or various approaches to beginning reading which used t.o., some of whom were authors of rival approaches, and a number of other educationists and writers. Although this minority group consisted mainly of people relatively unfamiliar with i.t.a. in practice, it also included a certain number of officials from authorities in which i.t.a. was used quite extensively but who, nevertheless, were not convinced that i.t.a. was preferable to t.o. as a medium of beginning reading instruction. The views of this small group of experienced observers constitute an important piece of evidence which should not be lost sight of in the mass of mainly favourable evidence.

2.   Reading

The overwhelming conclusions of teachers and other knowledgeable observers was that infants using i.t.a. learned to read earlier, more easily, more happily and at a faster rate than similar children using traditional orthography. As the regularity of the sound-symbol relationship meant that the child's own attempts at reading unknown words were generally successful, frustrations were minimized and he soon gained a sense of achievement. Consequently, young children chose to read individually more often, read for longer periods of time and read many more books, which soon extended far beyond basic reading schemes to include a wide variety of story books and reference books, as well as comics, newspapers and magazines.

When i.t.a. was first introduced, teachers had feared that children might find difficulty in transfering from i.t.a. to t.o. Yet in this enquiry, without exception, every teacher who had actually seen children make this transition in reading reported that the children experienced no difficulty. This was one of the few points where the verbal evidence and research evidence diverged. Certain of the research results showed that children who had recently transferred from i.t.a. to t.o. scored less on t.o. tests than on the same tests administered earlier in i.t.a. The writer concluded that a drop of a few points in test scores, even when statistically significant, did not necessarily represent a functional set-back in reading. She was convinced that had a functional set-back in reading occurred, the experienced teachers who gave evidence would have noted it, and would not have hesitated to include it with the other disadvantages of i.t.a. which they reported. Accordingly, she considered the verbal evidence on this score to be irrefutable.

The effect on children's reading standards of having learned to read initially with i.t.a. was not nearly as pronounced after about three years as in the first year or two. About half the teachers considered that at eight or nine years of age the original i.t.a. children retained certain advantages over t.o. children; other teachers saw little difference between the two groups at this stage.

3. *Writing and spelling*

Experienced observers reported that children's spelling in i.t.a. was more frequently correct than when t.o. was the medium of instruction. Moreover, no teacher reported that children taught initially by i.t.a. were less able spellers in t.o. than children who had used t.o. from the beginning.

The comparative simplicity and regularity of i.t.a. spelling had given children confidence about their ability to spell any word they chose. The result had been a marked increase in the quantity and quality of children's free written work which had delighted teachers as much as, if not more than, the improved reading.

4. *Slow-learning children*

More than half the teachers who had used i.t.a. were convinced that children of all levels of intelligence made better progress in reading and writing with i.t.a. than with t.o. The remainder were divided between believing it to be most effective for the brightest or for the slowest children. Thus only a few teachers considered that i.t.a. had not helped the slowest children, while many regarded the reduction in the number of non-readers and struggling readers in infant classes as one of its principal advantages.

This was the second point on which the two kinds of evidence

differed to some extent. The research evidence suggested that i.t.a.
was more effective with bright than with dull children. Again,
the writer supported the teachers' conclusions. She pointed out
that in many of the reported researches this conclusion was based
on the results of t.o. tests administered to children who had not
transferred from i.t.a. to t.o.—results unacceptable as valid
measurements of reading attainment. Moreover, the progress
made in the early stages of reading by the slowest pupils while
clearly discernible to the teacher is often difficult to measure
objectively by tests. It is also interesting to note that Downing
(1969) has revised some of his earlier conclusions on this score
and now reports that i.t.a. does help slow learners.

5. *The advantages and disadvantages of i.t.a.*

The people interviewed in this evaluation were asked to comment
on the advantages and disadvantages of using i.t.a. In the majority
of cases the advantages mentioned far outweighed the disadvantages, the latter being more frequently expressed as doubts or
dangers than as disadvantages. In fact, more than half the infant
teachers who had used i.t.a. approved of it so thoroughly that
they could perceive no disadvantages. The most common
responses to this question were as follows.

a. Advantages

  i The use of i.t.a. makes the early stages of learning to
     read easier and more enjoyable for children. As a
     consequence most children learn to read earlier and in a
     shorter space of time than they could have been expected
     to do with t.o.

 ii Children soon find they can make successful attempts
     to read unknown words themselves, without help from
     teachers. As a result, young children choose to read
     individually more often than when t.o. was used, read
     for longer periods of time and read more books.

iii The books children read soon extend beyond a basic
     reading scheme into a wide variety of story books,
     information books and reference books, as well as
     comics, newspapers, magazines, and pamphlets.

 iv i.t.a. has brought about a reduction in the number of

non-readers and struggling readers in infant classes and so reduced the frustration and lack of confidence formerly experienced by children who found difficulty in reading with t.o.

v The comparative regularity of the sound–symbol relationship enables children to make good attempts at spelling any word for themselves. The result has been a marked increase in the quantity and quality of children's free written work. This beneficial effect on children's free writing was listed as one of the main advantages of using i.t.a. as frequently as was its effect on reading.

vi Children who learn to read and write easily and happily with i.t.a. tend to develop confidence and independence, and to show initiative and responsibility in other aspects of school life at an early age.

vii The early mastery of the skill of reading and writing, together with the independent and confident attitudes developed by children, lead to an increase in individual study and exploration which is in line with current discovery methods of learning.

viii Children's earlier acquisition of the skills of reading and writing helps them with other subjects, for example, mathematics and science.

ix Teachers find they have more time to devote to the needs of individual children and to aspects of the curriculum other than the language arts.

x The introduction of i.t.a. has stirred up an increased interest in reading among teachers.

xi Many parents have become more interested in their children's reading. This has led to closer co-operation between parents and teachers.

b. *Disadvantages*

i Certain people, including teachers, parents and local inspectors who were familiar with i.t.a. in practice, and who were also favourably disposed towards it, continued to have misgivings about the effect on the children of using i.t.a. in school while they were seeing t.o. in every other situation in the total environment outside school.

ii   Some parents reported the frustration experienced by children not yet ready to transfer from i.t.a. to t.o. when they attempted to read t.o. print at home in books, comics, newspapers and other printed materials. These same parents found it a disadvantage to be unable to give the help requested by their children who were reading or writing in i.t.a. at home.

iii There was general concern about the problems which arose when a family moved and a child who was not a fluent reader in i.t.a. had to attend a school in which only t.o. was used.

iv   Inspectors, as well as the teachers themselves, were aware of the danger of attempting to hasten children's transition in reading from i.t.a. to t.o. This situation was most likely to arise when slower infants were about to be promoted to those junior schools not favourably disposed towards i.t.a.

v   Teachers in charge of classes in which some children were still reading in i.t.a. while others had transferred to t.o. found themselves in extremely demanding situations, and certain of them cited this as one of the main disadvantages of i.t.a.

vi   In 1966 the quantity and variety of books and other reading materials printed in i.t.a. was small compared with all the early reading materials available in t.o. (Although by 1969 the position had greatly improved, this statement must still be considered as valid.)

6.   *The headteacher's basic question*

The section of the report relating to the verbal evidence concluded by squarely facing the headteacher's basic, practical question about whether the children in his school would be likely to benefit by a change from t.o. to i.t.a. The answer given is that, providing the staff support the change and that continuity of approach is fairly certain, a headteacher deciding to use i.t.a. as the initial medium for beginning reading can be confident that at the very least children are unlikely to suffer, and that 'there is a substantial body of evidence which indicates that most children will benefit in a variety of ways'.

The replies of those teachers who had used i.t.a. for a number of years, and who were also experienced in using various t.o. approaches to beginning reading, to two 'key questions' are of relevance here. Of 29 such headteachers, asked whether they would continue to use i.t.a. or return to t.o. not one expressed an intention of returning to t.o. Ninety class teachers of similar experience were asked whether, if they were appointed head-teacher of new schools, they would use t.o. or i.t.a. Eighty-seven indicated they would choose i.t.a., two said t.o. and one was undecided.

V CONCLUSIONS DRAWN FROM THE TOTAL EVIDENCE

Although the two kinds of evidence on which this report was based were evaluated by means of different techniques, by two people whose backgrounds, interests and beliefs were far from identical, the conclusions proved to be fairly consistent and to lead broadly in the same direction—that is towards a favourable impression of i.t.a. as a means of beginning reading with infants.

However, the authors considered that it would be unfortunate if the generally favourable tone of their report were taken to imply that the use of i.t.a. for beginning reading with infants was the final and only solution. They were conscious that only one new medium had been compared with certain traditional ways of using t.o., and that other media or other ways of using t.o. might be found to be equally or even more effective than i.t.a. Accordingly, one of their principal recommendations for future reading research was that a large-scale experiment, comparing the results of using a number of different approaches to beginning reading, including i.t.a., should be undertaken, and that many more of the classroom variables should be controlled than had been usual in former experiments. It was also concluded that a great deal of fundamental research into the early stages of learning to read was required, and that there was an urgent need for the production of more useful tests of early reading ability.

8 Colour Codes Compared with i.t.a.

A paper presented to the Seventh Annual Study Conference of the United Kingdom Reading Association at Durham, July 1970, and later published in Merritt, J. E. (ed.) 1971 READING AND THE CURRICULUM.

I   WRITTEN ENGLISH

If the written or printed form of the English language had one symbol, and only one symbol, to represent each of the sounds of the spoken language, it could be regarded as a completely regular code, having a one-to-one relationship between spoken sound and written symbol. With a written form of the language based on an alphabet of 26 letters and a spoken language consisting of 40 odd sounds, we are clearly a long way from this goal.

The relationship between a spoken language and its written form is exercised in two distinct processes, decoding and encoding. Decoding is reading: the process whereby the child or adult looks at the written symbols and recognizes them as sounds, words, phrases and so on of the spoken language which he understands. He may utter these sounds aloud or abstract their meaning silently. Encoding is writing: the process whereby symbols are recorded as visual representation of the spoken or non-verbalized language, in the form of sounds, words, sentences, information or ideas. With a regular code, mastery of the skills of both decoding and encoding would be simpler than is the case with an irregular code.

But written English is not a regular language, either in the decoding or the encoding sense. The different pronunciation of the letter *c* in 'cat' and 'cinema', or the different sounds attached to the letter *o* in 'on', 'rose', 'one' and 'women', are two examples of irregularities encountered in decoding. With regard to encoding process, consider the young child who wants to w a word containing the sound *ee*. He could find himself floundering over the choice of double *ee* as in 'see', *ea* as in 'clean', or a single *e* as in 'he'. Additional variations of spelling for this sound are also available in English, for example *ei* in 'ceiling' or *ie* in 'belief' and *e* combined with a silent *e* at the end of a word as in 'these'. Fortunately for the child, he may at that time be unaware of the complete range of alternatives. It is unnecessary to give further illustrations of how an irregular spelling system (or 'writing system' as linguists often prefer to term it) necessarily increases the difficulties of learning to read and write.

II TWO MAIN METHODS OF BEGINNING READING

As far as reading is concerned, our written language consists of two broad categories of words. First, there are those words which are regular and may be decoded fairly easily by the child who knows the code and can utter the sounds which the letters represent. (In order to simplify the main theme of this paper, the undoubted difficulty experienced initially by some children in mastering the technique of blending sounds together is being disregarded.) The famous or infamous words 'cat' and 'mat', as well as longer words such as 'fantastic', are examples of words which follow simple regular rules. This first category of words, usually described as 'phonic' words, can be considerably extended to include many more words which are considered to conform to more difficult rules. The British phrasing of the rule that a 'silent' or 'magic' *e* at the end of a word like 'cake' makes the ă say ā, or the American phraseology of the rule for words such as 'boat' and 'seat', that 'When two vowels go walking the first one does the talking', are instances of such rules.

In passing it is worth noting that some of these rules do not have such general applicability as teachers often imagine. Clymer (1963), for example, shows that of forty-five phonic generalizations most commonly taught in elementary schools in the U.S.A., only eighteen are of general utility in that they are applicable to all or a majority of the words the child is likely to meet. For example, the rule 'When a word begins with "wr" the "w" is silent' is a rule having '100 per cent utility' as there are no exceptions whatsoever. In contrast, the rule 'When words end with silent "e", the preceding "a" is long', has only 60 per cent utility: 60 per cent of words, such as the word 'cake', for example, conform to the rule, while 40 per cent, such as 'have', represent exceptions to the rule.

In contrast to the phonically regular words are others which are quite irregular, such as 'said' and 'would'—words which a child cannot be expected to decode. These are words which the teacher must first tell the child, and which will then require extensive practice until they are recognized instantly on sight. Moreover, many of the most commonly used words in our language fall into this category of irregular words, as can be seen from McNally and Murray's (1962) *Key Words to Literacy*. Here are found, among the 'thirty basic words accounting for more than one third of the running words met with in ordinary reading, junior or adult', irregular words like 'the', 'was', 'all', 'he', 'are', 'have', 'one' and 'said'.

It is the difference between the most appropriate modes of learning and teaching regular and irregular words which has been partially responsible for teachers' preferences for beginning reading tuition with either a phonic or a look-and-say method. Whichever is chosen as the initial method, it is clear that neither can serve as the sole method and that a fluent reader needs to have mastered both techniques.

Herein lies one of the main difficulties of an irregular code for the beginning reader. The pupil quickly appreciates, even if this is not put into words by his teacher, that there are unknown words which he can tackle with reasonable success on his own, and that there are others which do not respond to 'sounding out' and which he must either 'guess' or ask the teacher or a fellow-pupil to tell him. Even more seriously, the child has no means of knowing which of these two methods is applicable to the unknown word confronting him. The bright child, of course, in time devises a workable form of attack. It might include first trying phonic analysis and, if this fails, discarding it as inappropriate or supplementing it by recourse to contextual clues. The slower child frequently merely gives up.

III THE MOVEMENT TO SIMPLIFY THE CODE

Attempts to regularize the written code of English have a long history. Pitman and St. John (1969) for instance, discuss 'Four Centuries of Spelling and Alphabet Reform'. In many instances proposed innovations centred on spelling reform. It is only more recently that such reforms were viewed in the light of transitional codes aimed at easing the task of beginning reading, and intended to be discarded in favour of t.o. (traditional orthography) when the pupil had reached an appropriate stage of reading fluency.

In *Formulae For Beginning Reading Tuition* (Southgate 1968b)* the writer has defined 'media' currently being used or considered for the initial stages of learning to read. Such attempts to regularize the code are polarized in two main directions. First, there are codes which accept the 26-letter alphabet and the current rules of English spelling, and superimpose signals in the form of colours or diacritical marks as aids to pronunciations. These are termed 'signalling systems'. Secondly, there are 'simplified spelling systems' which are likely either to employ an alphabet of 40-odd characters or to regularize the spelling rules governing the use of the present 26-letter alphabet.

In this paper three signalling systems, in the form of colour codes, *Words in Colour* (Gattegno 1962), *Colour Story Reading* (Jones 1967) and *Reading by Rainbow* (Bleasdale 1966), and one simplified spelling system, the Initial Teaching Alphabet, usually referred to as 'i.t.a.' (Pitman 1959), are compared. It is not possible here to either fully describe or examine in detail all four media.[1] They will be appraised in general terms only, in the light of their effectiveness as media for beginning reading, that is as decoding devices, although their effectiveness as encoding devices will also be mentioned.

* The article mentioned here forms Chapter 9 of this book.

IV POSSIBLE ADVANTAGES AND DISADVANTAGES OF
    REGULARIZED MEDIA

A summary of the possible advantages and disadvantages of
using some form of regularized medium for beginning reading
tuition in preference to t.o. is likely to form a useful background
against which to examine these media. The following list of
advantages and disadvantages is similar to the one given in
Reading—Which Approach? (Southgate and Roberts 1970).

1. *Advantages*

a. A regularized medium, whether it takes the form of a signalling system or a simplified spelling system, usually makes the
earliest stages of learning to read easier for the child.
b. If the medium represents a complete code to pronunciation,
the child can learn to adopt one invariable technique for attempting to decipher new words, and the employment of this technique
is almost certain to guarantee success.
c. The use of simplified regularized media, in place of t.o., is
thus likely to lead to a number of beneficial effects for the child,
including the following:
    i. there is less likelihood of failure;
    ii. he soon experiences success, pleasure and satisfaction;
    iii. his desire to read and his interest in reading increases;
    iv. he more quickly becomes independent of the teacher.
d. The task of helping children to learn to read becomes less
arduous for the teacher, with the result that she has more time
to devote to other aspects of the curriculum and the special needs
of individual children.
e. If the medium provides a regular encoding device, children's
ability to express themselves freely in writing will be facilitated.
Simplified spelling systems which provide a one-to-one relationship between sound and symbol, or which approach closely to
this ideal, are likely to gain in this respect over signalling systems
which are usually concerned with decoding.
f. The more regular the medium the more likely is it to result
in an improvement in children's spelling. Again, simplified spelling systems are likely to show the greatest advantage in this

respect. Signalling systems, while not aimed specifically at improving spelling, may nevertheless do so by drawing attention to both the regularities and irregularities of t.o.

2. *Disadvantages*

a. Certain difficulties may be encountered by both the children and their parents when the medium of instruction differs greatly from the traditional spelling system in use outside school. The closer the appearance of the new medium to t.o. the less important is this difficulty likely to be. On this count, signalling systems may have the advantage over simplified spelling systems which employ numerous new characters.
b. The quantity and variety of reading materials published in new media may be limited.
c. The published reading materials may be restricted to a single set of books or apparatus, applicable only to a definite method and with certain procedures which the teacher does not support. This disadvantage applies particularly to signalling systems.
d. Children who have to move to another school before they have transferred from the alternative medium to t.o. may experience difficulties.

V   COLOUR CODES AND i.t.a.

New media currently in use in British schools consist mainly of i.t.a. and the three colour codes already mentioned. The number of schools using these new media is certainly only a small proportion of those using t.o., but definite figures are not available. Warburton and Southgate (1969) found that 9·2% of all schools containing infant pupils were using i.t.a. to some extent with infants in 1966. This percentage has probably increased since then, but the extent of the increase is a matter for conjecture. No accurate information has been published regarding the number of schools using the various colour codes, although one would estimate their combined total to be less than that of schools using i.t.a.

Some of the principal similarities and differences between the three colour codes and i.t.a. are summarized in the table overleaf.

A COMPARISON OF THREE COLOUR CODES WITH i.t.a.

Approach / Author	WORDS IN COLOUR Gattegno, C. (1962)	COLOUR STORY READING Jones, J. K. (1967)	READING BY RAINBOW Bleasdale, E. and W. (1966)	i.t.a. Pitman, J. (1959)
Medium	A signalling system—using 47 different colours for letters.	A signalling system—using a few black letters, but most letters in 3 colours or on coloured background shapes.	A signalling system—⅓ of letters in 3 colours, and the rest in black.	A simplified signalling system—in the form of an augmented alphabet.
No. of sounds identified	47	42	(Number not identified)	44
Regularity of code 1. Decoding	1. Absolute regularity, one-to-one relationship.	1. Not an entirely complete code—2 signals—shape and colour needed for many letters; also some danger signals.	1. A partial code—not always consistent.	1. Almost a completely regular decoding device.
2. Encoding	2. As with t.o.—including its irregularities.	2. As with t.o.—including its irregularities.	2. As with t.o.—including its irregularities.	2. An almost completely regular encoding system.
Beginning method	Phonic (synthetic)	Phonic (analytic)—but Jones says look-and-say and phonic.	Phonic (synthetic)	Can be used with any method or any combination of methods.

Coloured wall charts, 3 children's basic books 1 story book in black type, worksheets, etc., in black. Only these materials to be used.	—3 children's basic books and activity kit of illustrations and games, all in colour. Other reading materials in black t.o. can be used alongside.	—4 children's basic books 2 supplementary readers, all in colour. Materials in black t.o. could probably be used towards end of scheme.	—10 or more Reading Schemes. Almost 1,000 titles including mathematics, information, story books, etc. Only i.t.a. materials to be used until the transition stage.
Procedures Very formal throughout. Class and group instruction at first. Directed exercises, including dictation.	Less formal than other 2 colour codes. Begins with stories read to children. Children's books require teacher direction and the symbols need to be taught.	Formal teaching required for the early books. Teaching activities suggested for mastering the sounds of the letters.	The teaching and learning procedures can be as formal or as informal as the teacher chooses. Teacher has absolute freedom of choice.
Approximate estimates of range of reading attainments Scheme covers *all* the 274 sound–symbol relationships of English. The child is learning to spell as well as read. Estimated R.A. of 9–10 at end of course—possibly higher.	Total vocabulary of 3 children's books is only 121 words —although supplementary work may have extended this total. Thus—only an introduction or aid to beginning reading.	Estimated level of Book 4— R.A. of 7 or $7\frac{1}{2}$	Average R.A. of approximately 8 on t.o. tests just after transfer from i.t.a. to t.o.

1.   *The medium*

The colour codes are all examples of signalling systems. They retain the 26-letter alphabet and the accepted spelling patterns of English, and all use colours to varying extents as signals to pronunciation. In *Words in Colour* Gattegno identifies 47 sounds in the English language and, by employing different shades and tints of the basic colours, as well as two-coloured letters, has produced a colour code of 47 colours, one for each sound. On his charts all the letters are coloured, none being black.

In *Colour Story Reading* Jones identifies 42 sounds. The colour code consists of black, together with red, blue and green. The majority of the letters are printed in the latter three colours, while a few are in black against the normal background of white paper. In addition, certain of the single letters or groups of letters are printed in black on red, blue and green backgrounds in the shape of a square, a circle and a triangle.

In *Reading by Rainbow* Bleasdale does not mention the number of sounds identified in English, as this colour code is clearly not aimed at providing signals for each sound. Approximately two-thirds of the letters are black; the remainder are blue, red or yellow.

i.t.a. is an example of a simplified spelling system, in the form of an augmented alphabet. Twenty-four of the 26 letters of the alphabet are retained; the letters x and q being discarded. Twenty additional characters make up the complete total of 44 characters which comprise the alphabet. Many of the 'new' characters consist of two t.o. letters which have been ligatured, for example, i and e or c and h joined together. Pitman (1959) states that i.t.a. leaves 50% of t.o. words virtually unchanged while a further 10% have only minor modifications such as the omission of an 'e' from the word 'have'.

2.   *The regularity of the code*

a.   *Reading* (i.e. decoding)
Words in Colour is a complete colour-code in which the colour of every letter or group of letters indicates the pronunciation.

It is also an absolutely consistent code with no deviations from the invariable rule that a letter or group of letters printed in a certain colour represents a particular sound. This code thus fulfils one of the main criteria suggested by the writer, as it presents the pupil with an invariable rule for decoding unknown words.

Colour Story Reading, while providing signals to the sounds of the majority of letters and words is not a complete code in the sense of *Words in Colour*, nor does it achieve absolute regularity. With 44 of its 53 colour symbols the child must look at both letter-shape and colour in order to know how to pronounce it; with the nine black letters on coloured background shapes, recognition of the background shape is sufficient to establish the relevant sound. The 53 symbols of this code thus provide the child with accurate and, in two distinct ways, consistent, clues for decoding. However, the inclusion of black letters on the ordinary background of white paper, for example, the *ai* in 'said' and the *a* in 'was' causes the code to diverge from the role of providing a clue to pronunciation. Such letters act only as danger signals, alerting the child to the fact that these letters are not to be pronounced as might be expected. Thus *Colour Story Reading* may be considered as a partial code which is fairly but not entirely complete. It gives the child clues to the pronunciation of a majority of the new words he may encounter but only supplies him with danger signals for a number of our common irregular words.

Reading by Rainbow needs also to be classified as a partial code, but one much less complete than the code of *Colour Story Reading*. The use of coloured letters is confined to a few of the more common rules which cause children difficulty: for example, letters printed in yellow to indicate they are silent letters, and the use of a blue *d* to distinguish it from a black *b*. While there is no doubt that such devices do help beginning readers to master certain irregularities of written English, a code incorporating only a few simple rules does not constitute a complete colour code. It cannot and does not overcome the child's dilemma about which words he can 'sound out' and which are look-and-say words. Neither is *Reading by Rainbow* entirely consistent within its own limited code: for example, although two blue *o*'s are used for the sound found in the middle of the word 'took', the words 'good' and 'foot' are printed in black and termed 'look-and-say' words.

When i.t.a. is examined, it will be found that as far as decoding is concerned the general rule applicable is that each written symbol represents one sound. This rule is not absolutely consistent as it is in *Words in Colour* where the same colour invariably denotes the same sound, but deviations from complete regularity are of a minor nature. For example, double consonants are retained in such words as 'little' and 'sitting' and the letter *y* is pronounced in two different ways at the beginning and end of words like 'yes' or 'silly'. Neither is a special character employed for the indeterminate vowel sound, as found for example in the words 'the', which can only be learned as a 'look-and-say' word.

In summing up on how these four approaches provide pupils with an infallible and completely regular decoding device, the writer would rank them as follows:

(1st) *Words in Colour* is an absolutely complete and regular code;

(2nd) *i.t.a.* is an almost complete and regular code;

(3rd) *Colour Story Reading* provides two different kinds of colour clues relating to a majority of English words but does not supply direct clues to the pronunciation of a number of irregular words;

(4th) *Reading by Rainbow* does not attempt to supply a complete decoding device, but employs a minimum of colour clues to help overcome certain common difficulties.

b. *Encoding* (i.e. writing)

These four new media were primarily designed to help children to learn to read more easily, yet a brief word ought to be said about their effect, if any, on children's free written work.

A simplified spelling system, by its very nature, must make it simpler for children to put down in writing the ideas they wish to express. By eliminating all or most of the irregularities found in t.o., a barrier to spontaneity of free expression in writing is removed. The result is that the child's confidence about expressing himself in writing is not undermined. Thus, one of the main

advantages of i.t.a. as reported by teachers, observers and researchers—for example, Downing (1964d and 1967a), Harrison
(1964), Sceats (1967), Warburton and Southgate (1969) and
Southgate (1970)—is a marked increase in the quantity and
quality of children's free written work, with greater accuracy
in i.t.a. spelling than was formerly experienced with t.o.
spelling.

In contrast, none of the signalling systems mentioned can be
considered specifically as encoding devices. For example, when
Words in Colour is used as the medium for beginning reading,
Gattegno does not suggest that children's free writing should be
encouraged. The children are expected to carry out written exercises concerned with the sound combinations they are currently
being taught. In this way, as they learn to read they are also
learning to spell in t.o., including the many variations of spelling
for identical sounds. By the end of the course, if Gattegno's
methods have been followed closely, a child would be able to
read and spell the entire 274 sound–symbol relationships identified
by Gattegno in the English language. How this affects children's
written expression in the long run would depend on the influence
and inspiration of the teacher, in that part of the school day not
devoted to reading tuition.

The preceding sentence is equally applicable to *Colour Story
Reading* and *Reading by Rainbow*. Neither is intended as an encoding device. A child's free written work would still be in t.o. and
the standards reached would depend largely on the teacher's
expectations, help and encouragement. Nevertheless, a child
whose attention has been drawn to the regularities and irregularities of English spelling, either by the use of a colour code or
by phonic training, will be likely to be more interested in the
spelling of words, and consequently a better speller, than the
child who has learned to read largely by a look-and-say method.
In this respect children who have used a colour code for beginning
reading should find spelling less of a deterrent to free writing than
children whose reading and writing experiences have been confined solely to ordinary t.o. accompanied by only limited phonic
training.

3. *Method*

Words in Colour employs a synthetic phonic method; that is individual letter sounds are taught first and are later combined to form regular words. *Reading by Rainbow* also begins in this way and should therefore be similarly classified. *Colour Story Reading* must also be counted as a method which begins with phonics. However, although the first book commences with the sounds made by various objects (for example, Sam the snake says 's'), the writer is inclined to regard it as basically employing an analytic phonic method, in which the word is the basic unit which the child analyses into its component parts.

With i.t.a., in contrast, the teacher can use any method he prefers. Most teachers in Britain have tended to begin reading in i.t.a. with a look-and-say method. Warburton and Southgate (1969), for instance, found only one teacher in England who began using i.t.a. by teaching children the sounds of the characters. In the U.S.A. the reverse has been the case. The majority of schools began to use i.t.a. with a phonic method, although some found it a valuable medium for use with a look-and-say method, including the language-experience approach.

4. *Reading Materials*

When colour codes are employed for beginning reading, the range of available reading materials is generally limited. This is true of the three colour codes being examined.

In *Words in Colour*, materials printed in the colour codes are confined to twenty-nine large wall charts showing single letters, groups of letters and discrete words. The material to be used by the children, namely three basic books consisting of words similar to those on the wall charts, with the addition of unconnected sentences, and one story book, are all in black and white. The children's worksheets and word-building books are also in black and white. While learning to read by means of *Words in Colour*, children are expected to be restricted to these reading materials.

In *Colour Story Reading* three children's books and an activity kit of illustrations and games are printed in the colour code. The children's books consist of prose in the form of simple stories related to characters named after the vowels. In contrast to *Words in Colour*, the author suggests that other t.o. materials could be used alongside the colour code materials.

Reading by Rainbow also has a limited range of children's reading materials printed in the colour code: four children's books and two supplementary readers. In contrast to the two preceding colour codes, the continuous prose fairly soon reaches the level of interesting stories embodying a variety of characters. A simple version of the story of Red Riding Hood forms the final part of Book 2, while Books 3 and 4 include stories about pirates, penguins and various animals. Although no directions are given about whether or not t.o. should be used alongside the scheme, one would imagine that towards the end of the scheme this practice would be acceptable and possibly even desirable.

i.t.a. contrasts with the colour code approaches in the large amount of children's reading materials now obtainable in this medium. There are now about 1,000 titles of children's books printed in i.t.a. available in Britain. These include ten or more beginning reading schemes, of which a few are designed primarily as remedial schemes, as well as supplementary story books, reference books, mathematics books and various games and activities. Other books in i.t.a. are published in the U.S.A. Whilst this breadth and variety of children's reading materials is the direct opposite of the limitations imposed in this respect by *Words in Colour*, the two approaches have one common feature: children's initial reading experiences are expected to be limited to materials printed in the appropriate code.

5. Procedures

When the kinds of classroom regime which could be adopted with these four approaches are examined, *Words in Colour* stands out as the most structured. Very formal teaching procedures are laid down throughout the scheme, with the teacher as the focal point, giving class and group instructions. *Reading by Rainbow* also requires the teacher to instruct at first, although teaching activities are suggested for mastering the sounds of the letters and later in the scheme children would be likely to require less and less teacher guidance. *Colour Story Reading* possibly requires the least formal teaching procedures of the three colour codes. The stories which the teacher reads to the children before they are given their own reading books introduce an informal note. Nevertheless, any scheme which requires children to master sound–symbol relationships in the early stages, as do all three colour codes, cannot avoid placing the teacher initially in the role of instructor.

The use of i.t.a. allows the teacher to adopt formal or informal procedures as she chooses. The children can be 'taught', or they can 'discover' for themselves.

6. *Range of reading attainment*

Just as with t.o. reading schemes, so do schemes using new media attempt to cover vastly different amounts of ground, in terms of vocabulary content, complexity of skills and range of content of the reading materials. Accordingly, the average reading attainments of pupils who have completed various schemes using new media can show wide divergencies.

If learning to read is regarded as a continuous developmental process extending from infancy to adulthood, and necessitating mastery of different sub-skills, *Words in Colour* makes by far the greatest progress along this path in terms of mastery of decoding skills. A child who has completed this course will have learned, or at least met, the 274 sound–symbol relationships of English. He should then be in a position to decode literally any word he wishes to read. On the other hand, if no other reading materials have been allowed, the child's practice in reading and enjoying continuous prose will have been seriously limited. A child who has completed this scheme would be likely to achieve a Reading Age of at least 9–10 years on a test consisting of decoding skills. His ceiling may even be considerably higher. The level of his reading comprehension would depend largely on the skill with which his teacher had encouraged him to utilize his increasing decoding skills.

If *Words in Colour* takes children the furthest along the road of learning to read, *Colour Story Reading* takes them the least distance. The *total* vocabulary of the first three books is only 121 different words, although the child's vocabulary may well have been extended by some of the work which it is suggested should be undertaken alongside the scheme. Thus *Colour Story Reading* is best considered as an introduction or aid to beginning reading.

In its extent of coverage *Reading by Rainbow* comes somewhere between the preceding two colour codes. It introduces some of the phonic rules and helps children to tackle certain of the irregularities of t.o., as does *Colour Story Reading*. On the other hand, more continuous children's reading material is available than with *Colour Story Reading*. Children who have completed the *Reading by Rainbow* scheme should certainly be able to read the simple supplementary story books which accompany or follow the final basic books of many of our well-known t.o. reading schemes, a stage which is often equivalent to a Reading age of about $7\frac{1}{2}$ on both mechanical and comprehension reading tests. The better readers would no doubt score higher than this on standardized reading tests.

At the completion of an initial course of reading using i.t.a., the appropriate figures to consider are scores on t.o. tests. An abundance of research evidence is available on this point. An examination of the results of Downing's and other people's researches indicates that on tests of both decoding and comprehension skills an approximate Reading Age of 8 soon after transfer is about the norm.

VI SUMMARIZING THIS COMPARISON OF COLOUR
    CODES AND i.t.a.

The authors and inventors of the four new media which have been examined share one common attribute. They all believe that the irregularities of t.o. increase children's difficulties in beginning reading. This common belief led each author to devise a code which would abolish or diminish the inconsistencies of t.o. in the initial stages of learning to read. In each case the new code required the printing of special reading materials, which in turn resulted in a laying down of methods and procedures to be adopted and, in varying amounts, limitations on the use of other reading materials. These points are summarized in the Table on pages 122-3 and have been examined in greater detail in the relevant sections of this paper.

It has been noted that the use of ordinary t.o., whether a phonic or a look-and-say method is employed initially, causes the child the same difficulty; he is bound to encounter two kinds of words, regular and irregular, which require different modes of attack. Accordingly, one of the most important questions to ask regarding each new medium relates to the extent to which it succeeds in providing the child with a uniform method of decoding unknown words. Secondly, one should probe for evidence of complications or disadvantages, and equally of possible additional bonuses, which might accompany the solution to this problem.

Words in Colour employs a complete and absolutely consistent colour code, so that any child who masters it develops a uniform method of reading unknown words printed in this code. The exercises which form an integral part of the approach will help the child to recognize letters in black print and reinforce his knowledge of the sounds they represent; they will also give flexibility in analysing and recombining both phonemes and graphemes in a manner that will lead to an appreciation of t.o. spelling rules. To achieve this effect, the teacher's own flexibility of approach must be largely sacrificed. The teacher must be willing to follow the rules laid down for her guidance, to confine children's reading materials to a limited set of books and apparatus, and to divorce reading tuition in the early stages from many of the other activities of the class.

Colour Story Reading, although it does not provide either a complete code or an absolutely consistent method of attempting to decode unknown words, does supply a partial colour code which will help the child by overcoming some of the anomalies of ordinary t.o. and by drawing attention to certain of the phonic regularities and conventions of t.o. In contrast to *Words in Colour*, it provides only a brief introductory course to beginning reading; it allows the teacher freedom to utilize it as either supplementary or basic materials and to choose other reading materials for use alongside it, and it presents the child with colourful books.

Reading by Rainbow also provides only a partial code, much less complete than *Colour Story Reading* and not as consistent. Again it draws attention to certain phonic rules, but fails to remove entirely the child's dilemma of irregular sight words alongside regular words which can be 'sounded'.

Neither does i.t.a. provide an absolutely complete and regular code for decoding new words, as does *Words in Colour*, but it approaches much more closely to this level than does *Colour Story Reading* or *Reading by Rainbow*. It has certain advantages over *Words in Colour*, as a teacher can choose to use any method and any procedures, and can also select whatever reading schemes and supporting materials he considers most appropriate. i.t.a. also has one other important advantage over all three colour codes, as it comprises a fairly regular encoding system which teachers have found to be a definite incentive to children's free writing. This in turn makes it easier for reading and writing to arise from, and be integrated with, the total activities of the primary school.

On the other hand, with i.t.a. there are two drawbacks which certain teachers may think important and which do not apply to the three colour codes. First, with i.t.a. the alphabet used in school is different from the one used outside. The writer, however, does not consider this to be a drawback which need cause teachers concern (Warburton and Southgate 1969, and Southgate 1970). Secondly, children have eventually to transfer from i.t.a. to t.o. both in reading and spelling, a problem which does not exist with the colour codes, as children use black print in t.o. alongside the colour code. While in normal circumstances the stage of transfer from i.t.a. to t.o. does not appear to cause children difficulty (see Southgate 1970), it may do so if the transition is unduly hastened or if the child has to be transferred suddenly to a school which uses only t.o.

This brief appraisal of four new media, three colour codes and i.t.a., shows that each has certain advantages over the use of ordinary t.o., although the advantages vary between the media. Any teacher who is convinced that the irregularities of the traditional spelling system of English is a hindrance to children who are learning to read and write would be failing in his professional capacity if he omitted to examine these approaches carefully. If the teacher also considers it important to find a simplified encoding system for children, if he wishes to encourage children's free writing from the beginning and to provide opportunities for individualized, discovery methods of learning, he cannot fail to note that i.t.a. fulfils these criteria while the colour codes do not set out to do this.

In this appraisal, it has also been noted that as well as advantages each new medium has certain features which different teachers will consider to be drawbacks. Whether to use a new medium in preference to t.o., and if so which one to select, is a personal choice to be made by the staff of a school. They cannot make it until they have listed their own criteria of assessment according to their own priorities regarding children's acquisition of the skills of reading and writing, against the framework of their total beliefs, aims and plans regarding the whole sphere of primary education.

ADDENDUM

1.   The principles underlying *Words in Colour* and the ways in which it should be used are fully explained in:

GATTEGNO, C. (1962b) *Words in Colour: Background and Principles.* Reading: Educational Explorers.

GATTEGNO, C. (1962c) *Words in Colour: Teacher's Guide.* Reading: Educational Explorers.

GATTEGNO, C. (1969) *Reading with Words in Colour: A Scientific Study of the Problems of Reading.* Reading: Educational Explorers.

Additional information about *Colour Story Reading* can be found in:

JONES, J. K. (1967b) *Colour Story Reading: A Research Report.* London: Nelson.

Part Three *Factors influencing reading progress*

9 Formulae for Beginning Reading Tuition

An article published in EDUCATIONAL RESEARCH, *Volume 11, No. 1, November 1968.*

I INTRODUCTION

Teachers who have read certain recently published research reports or accounts of new approaches to beginning reading—for example, Carrillo (1967), Cooper (1967), Dean (1966 and 1967), Downing (1967), Downing and Jones (1966), Fry (1967), Jones (1968), Lee (1967), Merritt (1967), Pont (1966), Roberts (1967) and Stott (1964 and 1966)—may have assumed that the selection of an approach is the most important factor affecting children's reading progress.

In this article attention is drawn to the numerous other factors which may exert much greater influence than the chosen approach. Researchers designing experiments with different approaches to reading in different schools or classes should consider the need to match many more of the variables than has usually been the case. And teachers whose attention is drawn to these interacting variables may be better able to evaluate the conclusions drawn from such experiments and to note, in particular, when only a minimum of factors affecting reading progress are controlled while other potent influences are ignored. At the same time, this emphasis on the numerous factors reacting within the reading situation may help teachers to realize that reading results can frequently be improved without the adoption of new reading schemes, books or apparatus.

II   TERMINOLOGY

We cannot usefully consider the tuition-learning situation unless
we clearly define our terms. Certain terms referring to the early
stages of reading tuition are currently employed with different
connotations, which adds to the difficulty of assessing the claims
of rival approaches. In an attempt to avoid such ambiguity, the
following terms are employed in this article according to the
definitions and descriptions given.

A.   *Medium*

The word 'medium' is used to mean the form of written and
printed symbols which represents the spoken language. Media
currently being used, or considered for use, in the early stages of
learning to read, may conveniently be divided into three broad
categories, although in some cases there is a certain amount of
overlap.

1.   't.o.'
't.o.' is the accepted abbreviation for 'traditional orthography'
which refers to the normal usage of our 26-letter alphabet when
it is employed according to the accepted rules of the English
spelling system.

2.   'Signalling systems'
A 'signalling system' is the term suggested for any written or
printed code which, while employing the 26-letter alphabet and
the traditional rules of English spelling, superimposes on the
letters certain distinguishing features. Some or all of the letters,
for instance, may be printed in colours other than black. Alternatively, differentiating marks, such as a line above a vowel which
has a long sound, or a stroke through a silent letter, can be superimposed on the letters. Such marks are generally termed 'diacritical marks'. Both the colours and the marks are intended to
act as signals regarding the pronunciation of letters and digraphs.
The aim is usually to produce either an absolutely regular code
or one with a close approximation to perfect regularity.

The originators of such signalling systems, while being willing to accept our alphabet and the irregularities of our spelling system for normal reading and writing, are attempting to simplify this code for the beginning reader, in the initial stages. Accordingly, the signals are designed only as temporary props to be discarded when fluency in reading simple materials is attained.

Gattegno's (1962) *Words in Colour* and Fry's (1964) *Diacritical Marking System* represent two examples of these contrasting types of signalling systems. A third system, Jones' (1967) *Colour Story Reading* illustrates the use of both colour and differentiating marks; the letters are printed in four colours while, in addition, certain black letters are superimposed on coloured squares, circles and triangles.

3. 'Simplified spelling systems'

Media classified as 'simplified spelling systems' can incorporate changes in, or additions to, the traditional alphabet, changes in the spelling rules or both.

Pitman's (1959) Initial Teaching Alphabet, usually abbreviated to 'i.t.a.', is an example of a simplified spelling system which retains 24 of the traditional letters of the alphabet, augmented by 20 new characters, so that the main spelling rule employed follows a one-to-one relationship between spoken sound and written symbol. Absolute regularity of sound–symbol relationship has not been attempted, since, to ease the transition to traditional spelling, a few examples of written symbols represented by different sounds and sounds represented by different characters have been retained.

A contrasting form of simplified spelling system is exemplified by Wijk's (1959) *Regularized Inglish*, in which the 26-letter alphabet and the regular rules of English spelling are retained while the spelling irregularities are reduced or abolished. This particular simplified spelling system, however, has not yet been tried as a medium for the initial teaching of reading in Britain.

B. *Materials*

The medium chosen to represent the written form of the spoken language is utilized in the preparation of reading materials designed to help children to learn to read. The term 'reading materials' includes not only basic reading schemes with all their supporting supplementary books, apparatus, games and pictures, but also other printed books and publications of all kinds, as well as hand-written cards, labels, lists, charts, stories and every form of written letters and words.

C. *Method*

In practice and in the literature on the teaching of reading, the word 'method' has tended to be used in a somewhat narrow sense to represent two kinds of emphasis in beginning reading instruction. On the one hand are what Gray (1956) describes as 'global methods', in which the child is encouraged to recognize, as the initial basic units, whole words and sentences which have meaning for him. In the everyday phraseology of teachers and most educators, global methods are mostly referred to as 'look-and-say' methods.

On the other hand, there are the 'phonic methods' in which the initial emphasis is on encouraging the child to equate printed or written symbols (i.e. graphemes) with spoken sounds (i.e. phonemes). The teacher's first concern is that the child should realize that there is a direct relationship between letters and sounds and that learning the code will enable him to read unknown words. A teacher using a phonic method can begin by teaching the sounds of single letters which are then blended together to form short regular words, or the introduction may be to whole words which are later analysed into separate sounds.

In practice, the irregularities of English spelling have been partially responsible for leading the majority of teachers to employ both methods, in what is usually termed an 'eclectic approach' to reading. The main variations are generally represented by the selection of one of these methods for use in the initial stages, and by the timing of the introduction of the other method in the reading programme.

Accordingly, although the word 'method' has a wider connotation in everyday language, it is suggested that it is retained in this narrower, but professionally accepted sense, to refer to ways of beginning reading which are 'look-and-say' or 'phonic'. The 'method' used for teaching beginning reading is usually very closely linked in classroom practice with what is described by the term 'procedure'.

D. *Procedure*

The word 'procedure' is being adopted to include and extend what is meant in ordinary usage by the word 'method', that is 'method of procedure'. The term 'procedure' includes, among other factors, the following:

a. the grouping of children for the purpose of learning to read. The whole class may be considered as a homogeneous unit, two or three large reading groups or many small groups may be formed, or each child may be regarded as an individual learning unit;

b. the varying roles of the teacher and the pupil, as exemplified in the ratio of teacher-instruction to pupil-participation in, and initiation of, the learning process;

c. the formality or informality of the working relationships between teacher and pupil—which is closely related to the preceding two points;

d. the emphasis given to pre-reading activities;

e. the timing of the introduction of the more formal beginning of reading;

f. the emphasis on other linguistic skills, such as speech and writing, in relation to learning to read;

g. the rigidity or otherwise of the time spent on reading and literacy training: that is, the extent to which it is confined to definite lesson periods or spreads throughout the day;

h. the use made of various reading materials, exemplified in a dependence on a basic reading scheme, the use of a variety of books and printed materials, or an emphasis on words originating from the children and written by the teacher or pupils.

E. *Reading formulae*

The ways in which the children in any group are initiated into reading skills represent a basic plan consisting of a combination of many influences. It develops from the beliefs about reading prevalent in the school and is exemplified in the medium, materials and method selected, as well as the way in which the materials are used and the learning takes place within the broad framework of classroom procedure. In the literature on reading and in practice there is little evidence of one special word or phrase being utilized to describe this master-plan. The word 'approach' is sometimes employed in this context but its connotation is neither sufficiently broad nor precise for what is required here. The term 'reading formula' is therefore being adopted to represent the combination of all those factors comprising the total tuition-learning situation within the class.

It is clear that formulae for reading progress are not confined to a few basic equations from which teachers may make their selections. There is infinite variety in the formulae developed by different teachers. In every formula, the numerous factors are capable of being emphasized or altered, and sometimes one particular item carries greater weight than the others. Certain formulae are fairly rigid; others are more flexible. Two examples of contrasting formulae may serve to clarify this point.

Gattegno's (1962) *Words in Colour* represents a quite rigid formula for beginning reading. It springs from two main beliefs: firstly, that most of the initial difficulties in learning to read arise from the irregularities of our spelling system and can be overcome by the use of a 'signalling system' based on colour; and, secondly, that initial mastery of reading skill should not be left to develop from a child's individual interests and explorations but should be the result of definite instruction and guidance from the teacher. Accordingly, this particular formula for beginning reading instruction uses a colour code as a signalling system, with a defined and limited range of materials, employs a synthetic phonic method and lays down precise instructions for formal teaching procedures which must, to a large extent, determine the entire classroom procedure.

The 'language-experience approach' to reading, as it is termed in the U.S.A., is an example of a formula which has been in use for many years in certain so-called 'progressive' infant schools in Britain, without ever acquiring a definite title. It is based on the belief that the spoken words of the child are those likely to have the highest motivational value for him, and consequently, those which should form his initial reading and writing vocabulary. This formula can utilize any medium but it must necessarily embody a 'look-and-say' method in the initial stages. The materials will vary from class to class, and even from child to child, but they will usually be hand-written materials at first and will later include a wide variety of printed books and other materials. The adoption of such a formula must necessarily lead to very different classroom procedures from those prevalent where *Words in Colour* is being used.

F. *Approach*

The phrase 'approach to reading' has recently been employed in a variety of ways without acquiring any useful definition. For example, it is sometimes used to mean 'medium', 'method', or 'reading scheme'. It is suggested that this phrase should be utilized only in a general sense to mean the manner in which reading is taught or the ways in which children learn to read. It will thus have a broader connotation than if it were used as a substitute for any single factor such as method or reading scheme, and will often refer to a combination of a limited number of factors. The term 'approach' can thus be employed in a much less precise sense than the term 'formula'.

III FORMULAE FOR READING PROGRESS

A. *The relative importance of the variables*

A child's reading progress, although determined to a certain extent by factors within himself, such as age, sex, intelligence, interest, and motivation, and by other factors relating to his home background, such as the socio-economic level of his parents, their reading habits and their interest in his school progress, is also profoundly affected by the total tuition-learning situation within his school, and more particularly, within his class.

Researchers who are planning experiments relating to

beginning reading usually attempt to match either individual children, or groups of children, on certain of the personal and social variables. Matching is rarely undertaken, however, with more than a few of the important classroom variables, as pointed out by Vernon (1967), with reference to Downing's (1967) first i.t.a. experiment. Indeed, research workers sometimes appear unaware of the numerous factors within the school which do substantially affect children's reading progress. The great measure of freedom accorded to British teachers and the flexibility of infant educational practices, in contrast to the more regular and formalized patterns of work in many other countries, for instance in the U.S.A., greatly increases the number of variables operating within the classroom.

While accepting the importance of individual differences in children and their relevance to scholastic progress, it must be stressed that the average level of reading progress in any class depends, to a large extent, on the interaction of the many factors peculiar to that class which comprise the formula for reading tuition-learning. In experiments in different schools and classes, even when children are carefully matched for age, sex, intelligence, linguistic ability, socio-economic background, and so on, unless the total formulae adopted for reading tuition in the respective classes is identical, the results cannot be considered as strictly comparable.

Experimenters obviously cannot control or match all of the relevant factors present in the reading tuition-learning situation. Some order of priority of variables must therefore be established, with those factors most closely affecting progress at the top of the list. Unfortunately, little reliable evidence on the relative importance of the variables is available, although two particular factors appear to me to be crucial.

I think that the most decisive factor influencing children's reading progress is the beliefs and attitudes of the staff about the importance of reading. In those schools in which the staff consider reading of prime importance and favour an early beginning to reading tuition, a strong reading drive (Southgate 1965) is permanently in force and most children do learn to read early and well, almost regardless of the media, methods, materials, or procedures adopted. In those infant schools in which the staff are convinced of the value of delaying the beginning of reading tuition, little or no reading drive is in force and children's reading progress in their first year or two at school is noticeably slower. There is an obvious difference in the reading standards of children in two such infant schools, even though they are in similar areas and have children of equal ability.

I consider that the second most important variable affecting children's reading progress is the teacher's competence in reading tuition, represented by a combination of ability, beliefs, training and experience. The importance of teacher competence is endorsed by most headteachers, advisers and inspectors, and there is also a certain amount of research evidence to support this view: for example, Chall and Fieldman (1966), Harris and Serwer (1966), Malmquist (1958), and Morris (1966). Other factors influencing reading progress are clearly the media, methods, materials and procedures adopted. Yet I am convinced that competent teachers of reading, with a strong belief in the importance of reading, produce good results whatever combination of the above factors is utilized in their classes.

Within the variables of medium, method and materials, research results do not clearly indicate which are the most or least influential. Proponents of new media inevitably consider the medium to be the most vital factor. They are convinced that the anomalies of our irregular spelling system are the greatest hindrance to the initial acquisition of reading skills and that the use of a simplified code will accelerate reading progress. Supporters of one or other of the two broad divisions of reading methods likewise see the choice of method as the most crucial factor. The authors of published reading schemes frequently imply that the selection of appropriate reading materials is the most important decision which teachers must take.

Yet, within the framework of 'the three Ms', materials, I think, constitute the least important factor. Certain researchers, such as Downing (1967b), Downing and Jones (1966), Latham (1967), Milne (1966), and Robinson (1966), have considered reading materials a highly significant feature of the reading environment. Even so, they have not been able to control their groups' total exposure to the printed and written word, but have confined themselves to matching basic reading schemes. In fact, British infant schools just do not have infant classes in which children learn to read entirely by means of one set of books or apparatus, without supportive materials. Indeed, in many cases the words found in the early stages of a basic reading scheme may form only a small proportion of the actual printed and written vocabulary with which the child is in contact during his time in school.

In laboratory experiments, the matching of reading materials would be both desirable and practicable. In experiments in most British infant classes, particularly when more progressive procedures are in force, it would be quite impossible to match reading materials, and it may well be unnecessary, since the procedures themselves may be much more potent elements than the actual words employed.

Deciding on the relative importance of medium and method is more difficult, since they are often closely interwoven. Probably medium should be given first priority, as the use of a regular medium undoubtedly simplifies the initial task of learning to read. Yet the combination of a phonic method with an irregular medium in certain schools sometimes results in better reading than the use of a 'look-and-say' method with a regular medium.

Placing the various aspects of procedure in an order of priority, individually or in relation to the three Ms, is an even harder task than ranking medium, method and materials. The timing of the introduction of the more formal beginnings of reading can certainly be singled out as a most important factor, however.

Several researchers have also considered the time spent on reading tuition and practice to be important. For example, in their experiments in the U.S.A., Fry (1966), Hale, Beltramo and Muehl (1967), Harris and Serwer (1966), Mazurkiewicz (1965), McCracken (1966), Robinson (1966), Ruddell (1966), and Tanyzer and Alpert (1966), have prescribed the amount of time to be devoted to reading instruction and supportive activities. Moreover, the experiments of Harris and Serwer (1966) led them to conclude that the time devoted to reading instruction was an important variable affecting reading progress and possibly more important than the instructional methods employed. In contrast, in British schools the time devoted to reading activities is not usually controlled. This may be because there is much less direct instruction, and greater emphasis on incidental learning and individual guidance throughout the day, than in the U.S.A. Research has so far given no clear guidance as to whether the latter procedure in British infant schools is more or less effective than direct instruction.

It is difficult to judge how the other aspects of procedure should be ranked. There are instances of classes using entirely different forms of procedure and achieving equally good results. Individual learning and class teaching, formal and informal regimes, learning to read through writing or without writing a word, have, on occasions, all given commendable reading results.

This should not discourage the researcher who is setting up reading experiments in different primary schools from attempting the task. There is an obvious need for many small experiments to establish the relative importance of the variables. Meanwhile, until more is known on this point, it is essential that the existence of the numerous relevant variables operating in infant classes should be recognised, and a more determined effort made to control or match them.

B. *The formula itself*

    Key to Abbreviations   RD = reading drive
                               TC = teacher competence
                         MM = medium
                         MD = method
                         ML = materials
                            P = procedure

Using the foregoing abbreviations, it is suggested that the formula for reading success in any class may be represented as follows:

Reading Progress = RD + TC + MM + MD + ML + P

Such a formula is not meant to imply that reading progress is merely the additive effect of the separate items. In practice a fusion takes place when the various factors are combined, with the result that the whole is different from the sum of the parts, just as in a chemical formula. Thus the formula for reading progress is only a simple way of expressing major influences at work in a dynamic situation. The items in this particular formula are arranged in order, according to my assessment of their importance, and each item should be preceded by a number to represent its weighting or choice of alternatives.

Each of the first two items needs weighting according to its position on a continuum, extending from strength to weakness. The third item, medium, could theoretically represent a selection made from 10 or 20 media but, in practice in Britain at the present time, the choice is confined to perhaps half a dozen media. Method could possibly be described in three broad categories, 'look-and-say', phonic or a combination of both, but a really useful description would entail many more divisions. For instance, a 'look-and-say' beginning may introduce phonics at varying stages in the reading programme or not at all, while phonic methods show considerable diversity and may begin with either an analytic or a synthetic approach. Thus it would not be out of the way to postulate a choice of eight or ten methods.

'Materials' can be sub-divided into basic reading schemes, library corner books, printed charts, cards and apparatus, home-made and hand-written materials, each varying in quantity and content. The final item 'procedure' is made up of perhaps ten or more sub-items, as suggested earlier, each having various weightings or choices, resulting in a large number of possible procedures.

It is obvious that the number of different formulae for reading progress in use in infant classes in Britain could quite easily number 100 and might very well extend beyond that number.

IV   IMPLICATIONS FOR FUTURE RESEARCH

If the concept of a formula for reading progress representing the total tuition-learning situation within a class is accepted, certain implications must follow for future research projects comparing different approaches to beginning reading in different schools and classes. The most obvious point is that, having matched children on a number of personal and social characteristics, to match, in addition, only two or three of the relevant factors in the tuition-learning situations, such as the medium of instruction and the basic reading scheme, results in an experimental design which is completely inadequate. The aim should be to match the total reading formulae of classes as closely as possible. Only the careful initial matching of a large number of variables, in their estimated order of effective priority, together with close observation and tight control of classroom practices throughout an experiment, can produce meaningful data about the variables under consideration.

Certain other implications follow the acceptance of this concept. For instance, many of the items in the formula, such as reading drive, teacher competence, methods and procedures, require subjective assessments by outside observers. This issue should not be shirked because of the subjective nature of the required assessments. Headteachers themselves are usually good judges of teacher ability. Many regular visitors to schools, such as advisers and organisers, develop powers of assessing most of the preceding variables and researchers should not hesitate to call upon their help. An experienced local education authority's infant adviser, for instance, could quite well assess reading drive in infant schools in the authority, on a five-point scale. Such an assessment could be supplemented by an attitude scale applied to the headteacher and members of the staff of certain schools.

Matching classes for most of the items in a reading formula although far from easy should not prove totally impossible. Different means would need to be devised for quantifying each item and sub-item in the formula but such a task goes beyond the scope of this article. However, early and detailed discussions between researchers and teachers taking part in experiments can help with categorizing methods and many of the items listed under procedure. Regular meetings at intervals throughout the duration of the research project can help to ensure that agreed methods and procedures are continued. For, as Morris (1966) and Chall and Fieldman (1966) note, teachers rarely do what they say they do.

Detailed planning of this nature, ensuring the continuance of specified reading formulae for an extended period, also requires regular visits to classes by skilled observers. Any team of researchers undertaking an experiment to compare different approaches to beginning reading should certainly include people experienced in observing reading in infant schools and preferably experienced in teaching reading. Such researchers would be welcomed by teachers into their classrooms and would be in good positions to notice divergences from agreed formulae and to rectify them before they could influence reading results.

This close co-operation between researchers and teachers in respect of classroom practices will demand an increase in the number of researchers in any one project, or a reduction in the number of schools taking part in an experiment, or both. In any event, a small experiment in which very close control is exercised over a large number of variables is more likely to produce valid results than a large-scale experiment which is more loosely designed and controlled.

V   CONCLUSIONS

Designing and conducting reading experiments in infant classes in Britain is complicated not only by the variety of existing practices but also by the informality of certain classroom regimes. Researchers planning such experiments need to be more aware of the numerous variables affecting reading progress within the total tuition-learning situations in classrooms, and of the variations of actual procedures in classes apparently working on similar lines.

Field experiments conducted in infant classes require much more detailed planning and tightly controlled execution than we have been accustomed to accept. It is not sufficient to match children for individual characteristics and variables in their social background, while giving only fleeting attention to what goes on in different classes. Only a meticulous analysis of the total formulae for reading tuition-learning within classes, careful matching of many more of these variables than has commonly been considered necessary, and frequent observations of procedures actually in force as the experiments continue, are likely to produce meaningful results for both the researcher and the teacher.

The use of clearly defined terminology and an appreciation of the many relevant factors operating in schools should make it easier for teachers to assess the results of experiments with different approaches to reading, and to realize that reading standards might be improved without necessarily adopting a different approach.

References

ANDERSON, I. H. (1964) 'Comparison of the reading and spelling achievement and quality of handwriting of groups of English, Scottish and American children.' *Co-operative Research Project No. 1903,* University of Michigan.

BIRCH, L. B. (1953) 'Comments on the article "An experimental evaluation of remedial education", by W. Curr and N. Gourlay.' *British Journal of Educational Psychology,* Vol. 23, No. 1, 56–57.

BLEASDALE, E. and W. (1966) *Reading by Rainbow.* Bolton: Moor Platt Press.

BOYCE, E. R. (1959) *The Gay Way Series.* London: Macmillan.

BREARLEY, M. and NEILSON, L. (1964) *Queensway Reading.* London: Evans.

BROWN, A. L. (ed.) (1967) *Reading: Current Research and Practice.* Edinburgh: Chambers.

CARRILLO, L. W. (1967) 'The Language-Experience Approach to the teaching of reading.' In DOWNING, J. and BROWN, A. L. (eds.) *The Second International Reading Symposium.* London: Cassell.

CARVER, C. and STOWASSER, C. H. (1963) *Oxford Colour Readers.* Oxford: Oxford University Press.

CASTLEY, D., FOWLER, K. and CARSTAIRS, S. (1958–61) *The McKee Platform Readers.* London: Nelson.

CHALL, J. and FIELDMAN, S. (1966) 'First Grade Reading: an analysis of the interactions of professed methods, teacher implementation and child background.' *The Reading Teacher,* Vol. 19, No. 8, 569–575.

CLEGG, A. B. (ed.) (1964) *The Excitement of Writing.* London: Chatto and Windus.

CLYMER, T. (1963) 'The Utility of Phonic Generalisations.' *The Reading Teacher,* Vol. 16, No. 4, 252–258.

COOK, D. L. (1962) 'The Hawthorne effect in educational research.' *Phi Delta Kappa,* December 1962, 116–122.

COOPER, M. G. (1967) 'The language-experience approach to reading.' *Reading,* Vol. 1, No. 2, 20–24.

DANIELS, J. C. and DIACK, H. (1956) *Progress in Reading.* Nottingham: University Institute of Education.

DANIELS, J. C. and DIACK, H. (1957) *The Royal Road Readers*. London: Chatto and Windus.

DANIELS, J. C. and DIACK, H. (1960) *Progress in Reading in the Infant School*, Nottingham: University Institute of Education.

DEAN, J. (1966) ' "Words in Colour".' In DOWNING, J. (ed.) *The First International Reading Symposium*. London: Cassell.

DEAN, J. (1967) 'Second Report on "Words in Colour".' In DOWNING, J. and BROWN, A. L. (eds.) *The Second International Reading Symposium*. London: Cassell.

DEPARTMENT OF EDUCATION AND SCIENCE (1967) *Children and their Primary Schools* (The Plowden Report). *Volume 1: The Report*. London: H.M. Stationery Office.

DEPARTMENT OF EDUCATION AND SCIENCE (1970) *Trends in Education*, Number 20 (October 1970). London: H.M. Stationery Office.

DIACK, H. (1963) *Reading and the Psychology of Perception*. Nottingham: Ray Palmer.

DOMAN, G. (1965) *Teach your Baby to Read*. London: Jonathan Cape.

DOWNING, J. A. (1962a) 'The relationship between reading attainment and the inconsistency of English spelling at the infants' school stage.' *British Journal of Educational Psychology*, Vol. 32, No. 2, 166–177.

DOWNING, J. A. (1962b) *To Be or Not to Be*. London: Cassell.

DOWNING, J. A. (1963a) 'Is a "mental age of six" essential for reading readiness?' *Educational Research*, Vol. 6, No. 1, 16–28.

DOWNING, J. A. (1963b) 'The Augmented Roman alphabet research—Interim report of experiments conducted in 1961–1962.' *British Psychological Society Bulletin*, Vol. 16, 50.

DOWNING, J. A. (1964a) *The i.t.a. Reading Experiment*. London: Evans.

DOWNING, J. A. (1964b) 'Learning to read: i.t. alphabet success.' *Times Educational Supplement*, 20 March 1964.

DOWNING, J. A. (1964c) Letter to the Editor of the *Bulletin of the British Psychological Society*, Vol. 17, No. 55, 37–38.

DOWNING, J. A. (1964d) *Examples of Children's Creative Writing from Schools using i.t.a.* (Reading Research Document No. 4). London: University of London, Institute of Education.

DOWNING, J. (1967a) *The i.t.a. Symposium*. Slough: National Foundation for Educational Research.

DOWNING, J. (1967b) *Evaluating the Initial Teaching Alphabet*. London: Cassell.

DOWNING, J. (1969) 'i.t.a. and Slow Learners: A Reappraisal.' *Educational Research*, Vol. 11, No. 3, 229–231.

DOWNING, J. (1971) 'i.t.a.—a review of ten years' research.' In MERRITT, J. E. (ed.) *Reading and the Curriculum*. London: Ward Lock.

DOWNING, J. and BROWN, A. L. (eds.) (1967) *The Second International Reading Symposium.* London: Cassell.

DOWNING, J. A. and GARDNER, K. (1962) 'New experimental evidence on the role of the unsystematic spelling of English in reading failure.' *Educational Research,* Vol. 5, No. 1, 69–76.

DOWNING, J. A. and JONES, B. (1966) 'Some problems of evaluating i.t.a.: a second experiment.' *Educational Research,* Vol. 8, No. 2, 100–14.

FERNALD, G. M. (1943) *Remedial Techniques in Basic School Subjects.* New York: McGraw Hill.

FLOWERDEW, P. and SCHONELL, F. *Happy Venture Library Books.* Edinburgh: Oliver & Boyd.

FRY, E. (1964) 'A diacritical marking system to aid beginning reading instruction.' *Elementary English,* May 1964.

FRY, E. B. (1966) 'First grade reading instruction using diacritical marking system, initial teaching alphabet and basal reading system.' *The Reading Teacher,* Vol. 19, No. 8, *U.S. Office of Education First Grade Reading Studies,* 667.

FRY, E. (1967) 'The diacritical marking system and a preliminary comparison with i.t.a.' In DOWNING, J. and BROWN, A. L. (eds.) *The Second International Reading Symposium.* London: Cassell.

GALT   *Key Words Self Teaching Cards.* (N.970 and N.971.) Cheadle: Galt.

GALT   *Basic Words Lotto.* (N.692.) Cheadle: Galt.

GALT   *Key Words Lotto.* (N.940, N.941 and N.942.) Cheadle: Galt.

GARDNER, K. (ed.) (1970) *Reading Skills: Theory and Practice.* London: Ward Lock.

GATTEGNO, C. (1962a) *Words in Colour.* Reading: Educational Explorers.

GATTEGNO, C. (1962b) *Words in Colour: Background and Principles.* Reading: Educational Explorers.

GATTEGNO, C. (1962c) *Words in Colour: Teacher's Guide.* Reading: Educational Explorers.

GATTEGNO, C. (1969) *Reading with Words in Colour: A Scientific Study of the Problems of Reading.* Reading: Educational Explorers.

GEORGIADES, N. J. (1963) 'Summary of research results.' *Pitman's i.t.a. Journal,* 5 December 1963, 8–9.

GLYNN, D. (1964) *Teach your Child to Read.* London: Pearson.

GOODACRE, E. J. (1967) *Reading in Infant Classes.* Slough: National Foundation for Educational Research.

GRASSAM, E. H. (1922, revised 1957) *The Beacon Readers.* London: Ginn.

GRASSAM, E. H. (1966) *Six Phonic Workbooks.* London: Ginn.

GRAY, W. S. (1956) *The Teaching of Reading and Writing—An International Survey.* London: Evans.

GRAY, W. S., MONROE, M., ARTLEY, A. S. and ARBUTHNOT, M. H. (1956) *The Happy Trio Reading Scheme*. Exeter: Wheaton.

HALE, C. R., BELTRAMO, L. and MUEHL, S. (1967) 'Teaching reading to the low group in the first grade—extended into second grade.' *The Reading Teacher*, Vol. 20, No. 8, 717.

HARRIS, A. J. and SERWER, B. L. (1966) 'The CRAFT Project: Instructional time in reading research.' In *Reading Research Quarterly*, Vol. 2, No. 1, 27–56. Newark, Delaware, U.S.A.: International Reading Association.

HARRISON, M. (1964) *Instant Reading: The Story of the Initial Teaching Alphabet*. London: Pitman.

INITIAL TEACHING ALPHABET FOUNDATION (1966) *i.t.a. Journal*, No. 9. London: Initial Teaching Alphabet Foundation.

JENKINSON, M. D. (ed.) (1967) *Reading Instruction: An International Forum*. Newark, Delaware, U.S.A.: International Reading Association.

JONES, J. K. (1967a) *Colour Story Reading*. London: Nelson.

JONES, J. K. (1967b) *Colour Story Reading: A Research Report*. London: Nelson.

JONES, J. K. (1968) 'Comparing i.t.a. with "Colour Story Reading".' *Educational Research*, Vol. 10, No. 3, 226–234.

JONES, W. R. (1965) *Step up and Read*. London: University of London Press.

KEIR, G. (1947) *Adventures in Reading*. Oxford: Oxford University Press.

KEIR, G. (1947) *Adventures in Writing*. Oxford: Oxford University Press.

KETTLES, P. and MACDONALD, R. A. D. (1949, revised 1963) *Vanguard Readers*. Edinburgh: McDougall.

LATHAM, W. (1967) 'i.t.a. research in beginners' classes in Britain.' In DOWNING, J. and BROWN, A. L. (eds.) *The Second International Reading Symposium*. London: Cassell.

LEE, . (1967) 'Writing the talking: an appraisal of "Words in Colour".' In BROWN, A. L., *Reading: Current Research and Practice*. Edinburgh: Chambers.

LYNN, R. (1963) 'Reading readiness and the perceptual abilities of young children.' *Educational Research*, Vol. 7, No. 1, 10–15.

MCCRACKEN, R. A. (1966) 'A two-year longitudinal study to determine the ability of first grade children to learn to read using the Early-to-Read i.t.a. programme.' (An interim report of the first year.) In MAZURKIEWICZ, A. J. (ed.) *i.t.a. and the World of English*. Hempstead, New York, U.S.A.: i.t.a. Foundation.

MCKEE, P., HARRISON, M. L., MCCOWEN, A. and LEHR, E. (1956) *The McKee Readers*. London: Nelson.

MCNALLY, J. and MURRAY, W. (1962) *Key Words to Literacy*. London: The Schoolmaster Publishing Co.

MAIL, A. (1968) *Springboard Readers*. London: Warne.

MALMQUIST, E. (1958) 'Factors related to reading disability in the first grade of the elementary school.' *Educational Research*, Vol. 1, No. 1, 69–72.

MAZURKIEWICZ, A. J. (1965) *First Grade Reading Using Modified Co-Basal Versus the Initial Teaching Alphabet*. Co-operative Research Project No. 2676. Bethlehem, Pennsylvania, U.S.A.: Lehigh University Office of Education.

MELSER, J. (1960) *Read it Yourself Books*. London: Methuen.

MERRITT, J. E. (1967) 'The S.R.A. laboratories: preview of a programmed course in reading.' In BROWN, A. L. (ed.) *Reading: Current Research and Practice*. Edinburgh: Chambers.

MERRITT, J. E. (ed.) (1971) *Reading and the Curriculum*. London: Ward Lock.

MILES, J. E. (1951) *Active Reading*. London: Ginn.

MILNE, A. (1966) *The Scottish i.t.a. Research*. Paper read at the Third International i.t.a. Conference, Cambridge University.

MINISTRY OF EDUCATION (1957) *Standards of Reading 1948–1956* (Pamphlet No. 32). London: H.M. Stationery Office.

MINISTRY OF EDUCATION (1959) *Primary Education*. London: H.M. Stationery Office.

MOORE, O. K. (1963) *Autotelic Responsive Environment and Exceptional Children*. Hamden, Connecticut, U.S.A.: Responsive Environments Foundation.

MORPHETT, M. V. and WASHBURNE, C. (1931) 'When should children begin to learn to read?' *Elementary School Journal*, Vol. 31, 496–503.

MORRIS, J. M. (1959) *Reading in the Primary School*. London: Newnes.

MORRIS, J. M. (1966) *Standards and Progress in Reading*. Slough: National Foundation for Educational Research.

MOXON, C. A. V. (1962) *A Remedial Reading Method*. London: Methuen.

MURRAY, W. (1964) *Key Words Reading Scheme*. Loughborough: Wills and Hepworth.

O'DONNELL, M. and MUNRO, R. (1949) *Janet and John*. Welwyn: Nisbet.

O'DONNELL, M. and MUNRO, R. (1951) *Janet and John Supplementary Books*. Welwyn: Nisbet.

O'DONNELL, M. and MUNRO, R. (1965) *Sounds for Reading*. Welwyn: Nisbet.

PARKER, D. H. (1958) *The S.R.A. Reading Laboratories*. Chicago: Science Research Associates.

PIERS, H. (1966) *Mouse Books*. London: Methuen.

PITMAN, J. (1959) *The Ehrhardt Augmented (40-sound 42-character) Lower-case Roman Alphabet*, London: Pitman.

PITMAN, J. (1961) 'Learning to read: an experiment.' *Journal of Royal Society of Arts*, Vol. 109, 149–180.

PITMAN, J. and ST. JOHN, J. (1969) *Alphabets and Reading*. London: Pitman.

PONT, H. B. (1966) 'An investigation into the use of the S.R.A. reading laboratory in three Midlothian schools.' *Educational Research*, Vol. 8, No. 3, 230–236.

PRINGLE, M. L. KELLMER and NEALE, M. D. (1957) 'A note on the use of the Schonell and Gates reading tests in the first year of the junior school.' *British Journal of Educational Psychology*, Vol. 27, 134–41.

RANDELL, B. (1966) *Methuen Caption Books*. London: Methuen.

REIS, M. (1962) *Fun with Phonics*. Cambridge: Cambridge Art Publishers.

ROBERTS, G. R. (1967) 'Towards a linguistic approach to reading.' *Reading*, Vol. 1, No. 1, 16–20.

ROBINSON, H. M. (1966) 'Effectiveness of i.t.a. as a medium for reading instruction.' In MAZURKIEWICZ, A. J. (ed.) *i.t.a. and the World of English*. Hempstead, New York, U.S.A.: i.t.a. Foundation.

ROSENBLOOM, P. C. (1961) 'Large-scale experimentation with mathematics curriculum.' In COLLIER, R. O. and ELLAM, S. M. (eds.) *Research Design and Analysis, 2nd Annual Phi Delta Kappa Symposium on Educational Research*, 1961, 1B, 11.

RUDDELL, R. B. (1966) 'Reading instruction in first grade with varying emphasis on the regularity of grapheme-phoneme correspondence and the relation of language structure to meaning.' *The Reading Teacher*, Vol. 19, No. 8, *U.S. Office of Education First Grade Reading Studies*, 655.

RYDER, E. (1957) *Stories For Me*. London: Macmillan.

SANDERSON, A. E. (1963) 'The idea of reading readiness: a re-examination. *Educational Research*, Vol. 6, No. 1, 3–9.

SCEATS, J. (1967) *i.t.a. and the Teaching of Literacy*. London: Bodley Head.

SCHOLL, G. T. (1960) 'The Reading and Spelling Achievement of a Group of English Children as Judged by the Standards on an American Achievement Test.' University of Michigan: unpublished doctoral dissertation.

SCHONELL, F. J. (1938) *The Happy Venture Readers*. Edinburgh: Oliver and Boyd.

SCOTTISH EDUCATION DEPARTMENT (1955) *Reading in the Primary School*. Edinburgh: H.M. Stationery Office.

SIMPSON, M. (1966) *Ready to Read Scheme*. London: Methuen.

SOUTHGATE, V. (1959) *Southgate Group Reading Tests: Test 1—Word Selection Test*. London: University of London Press.

SOUTHGATE, V. (1962) *Southgate Group Reading Tests: Test 2—Sentence Completion Test*. London: University of London Press.

SOUTHGATE, V. (1963) 'Augmented Roman Alphabet Experiment: An Outsider's Report.' *Educational Review*, Vol. 16, No. 1, 32–41.

SOUTHGATE, V. (1965) 'Approaching i.t.a. results with caution.' *Educational Research*, Vol. 7, No. 3, 83–96.

SOUTHGATE, V. (1966) 'Approaching i.t.a. results with caution.' *Reading Research Quarterly*, Vol. 1, No. 3, 35–56.

SOUTHGATE, V. (1967a) 'Approaches to Beginning Reading in Great Britain.' In JENKINSON, M. D. (ed.) *Reading Instruction: An international Forum.* Newark, Delaware, U.S.A.: International Reading Association.

SOUTHGATE, V. (with HAVENHAND, J. and HAVENHAND, I.) (1967b) *Sounds and Words Stories.* London: University of London Press.

SOUTHGATE, V. (1967c) 'The problem of selecting an approach to the teaching of reading.' In DOWNING, J. and BROWN, A. L. (eds.) *The Second International Reading Symposium.* London: Cassell.

SOUTHGATE, V. (1967d) 'Early reading.' In BROWN, A. L. (ed.) *Reading: Current Research and Practice.* Edinburgh: Chambers.

SOUTHGATE, V. (1967e) 'A few comments on "Reading Drive".' *Educational Research*, Vol. 9, No. 2, 145–146.

SOUTHGATE, V. (1968a) *First Words* (Books 1–12). London: Macmillan.

SOUTHGATE, V. (1968b) 'Formulae for beginning reading tuition.' *Educational Research*, Vol. 11, No. 1, 23–30.

SOUTHGATE, V. (1969) 'Structuring reading materials for beginning reading.' In STAIGER, R. C. and ANDRESON, O. (eds.) *Reading: A Human Right and a Human Problem.* Newark, Delaware, U.S.A.: International Reading Association.

SOUTHGATE, V. (1970a) 'The importance of structure in beginning reading.' In GARDNER, K. (ed.) *Reading Skills: Theory and Practice.* London: Ward Lock.

SOUTHGATE, V. (1970b) *i.t.a.: What is the Evidence?* Edinburgh: Chambers and London: Murray.

SOUTHGATE, V. (1971) 'Comparing colour codes with i.t.a.' In MERRITT, J. E. (ed.) *Reading and the Curriculum.* London: Ward Lock.

SOUTHGATE, V. and HAVENHAND, J. (1959) *Sounds and Words.* London: University of London Press.

SOUTHGATE, V. and ROBERTS, G. R. (1970) *Reading—Which Approach?* London: University of London Press.

STAIGER, R. C. and ANDRESON, O. (eds.) (1969) *Reading: A Human Right and a Human Problem.* Newark, Delaware, U.S.A.: International Reading Association.

STOTT, D. H. (1962) *Programmed Reading Kit.* Glasgow: Holmes.

STOTT, D. H. (1964) *Roads to Literacy.* Glasgow: Holmes.

SULLIVAN, M. W. (1963) *Programmed Reading.* Maidenhead: McGraw-Hill.

TANSLEY, A. E. (1961) *Sound Sense.* Leeds: Arnold.

TANYZER, H. J. and ALPERT, H. (1966) 'Three different basal reading systems and first grade reading achievement.' *The Reading Teacher*, Vol. 19, No. 8, U.S. Office of Education First Grade Reading Studies, 637.

TAYLOR, C. D. (1950) 'The effect of training on reading readiness.' In Scottish Council for Research in Education, Publication 34, *Studies in Reading, Vol. 1*, 63–80. London: University of London Press.

TAYLOR, J. and INGLEBY, T. (1960) *Let's Learn to Read*. London: Blackie.

TAYLOR, J. and INGLEBY, T. (1961) *Reading with Rhythm*. London: Longmans.

TAYLOR, J. and INGLEBY, T. (1965) *This is the Way I Go*. London: Longmans.

VERNON, M. D. (1967) 'Evaluations II.' In DOWNING, J. A. (ed.) *The i.t.a. Symposium*. Slough: National Foundation for Educational Research.

WARBURTON, F. W. and SOUTHGATE, V. (1969) *i.t.a.: An Independent Evaluation*. Edinburgh: Chambers and London: Murray.

WEBSTER, J. (1965) *Practical Reading: Some New Remedial Techniques*. London: Evans.

WIJK, A. (1959) *Regularized Inglish*. Stockholm: Almquist and Wiksell.

Index